Praise for
Do I Know God?

"Warm, fresh, and helpful, Tullian's insightful answer to the question 'Do I know God?' will be a guide and an encouragement to many."

—Os GUINNESS, author of *The Call*

"With wisdom, grace, and transparency, Tullian helps clear the sometimes uncertain path of knowing and following after God. I am thrilled to endorse this thoughtful work and trust you will find it equally engaging and helpful."

—RAVI ZACHARIAS, author of *Can Man Live Without God?*

"Many people are confused today as to whether we can truly know God. Is it possible to actually have a relationship with the Creator of the universe? This book by my former student Tullian Tchividjian makes it clear that we can have such certainty and how that certainty is possible. It is thoroughly biblical, well balanced, excellently stated and illustrated. May God use Tullian's volume to bring many to the wonderful assurance that God loves them in Jesus Christ."

—JOHN M. FRAME, J. D. Trimble Chair of Systematic Theology and Philosophy at Reformed Theological Seminary

"Tullian has written a good, simple, solid book on a crucial subject. Tullian wants you to know God and to know that you know God. Do you know God? This book can help you answer that most important of all questions. What better reason is there to spend money on buying a book—or time on reading it?"

> —MARK E. DEVER, senior pastor, Capitol Hill
> Baptist Church, Washington, DC

"This is a warm, personal book about assurance, about how we can know we have been redeemed by Christ. It is written with pastoral wisdom for a church often afflicted by deep currents of uncertainty and sometimes by faltering discipleship. It speaks to our time with biblical fidelity."

> —DAVID F. WELLS, Andrew Mutch Distinguished
> Professor of Historical and Systematic Theology
> at Gordon-Conwell Theological Seminary

"To know that you know God and God knows you is life's greatest source of peace, joy, and strength for the journey. Tullian takes strugglers by the hand and leads them with sure steps toward this certainty. Here is a book to be trusted and treasured."

> —J. I. PACKER, author of *Knowing God*

DO I KNOW GOD?

Finding Certainty in Life's Most Important Relationship

TULLIAN TCHIVIDJIAN

MULTNOMAH
BOOKS

Do I Know God?
Published by Multnomah Books
12265 Oracle Boulevard, Suite 200
Colorado Springs, Colorado 80921

All Scripture quotations, unless otherwise indicated, are taken from the Holy
Bible, English Standard Version, copyright © 2001 by Crossway Bibles, a publishing ministry of Good News Publishers. All rights reserved. Scripture quotations
marked (NIV) are taken from the Holy Bible, New International Version®.
NIV®. Copyright © 1973, 1978, 1984 by International Bible Society. Used by
permission of Zondervan Publishing House. All rights reserved.

Some names and minor details in stories have been changed to protect privacy.

Trade Paperback ISBN 978-1-60142-218-7
Hardcover ISBN 978-1-59052-936-2
eBook ISBN 978-0-307-56181-7

Published in the United States by WaterBrook Multnomah, an imprint of the
Crown Publishing Group, a division of Penguin Random House LLC, New York.

MULTNOMAH and its mountain colophon are registered trademarks of Penguin
Random House LLC.

Library of Congress Cataloging-in-Publication Data
Tchividjian, Tullian.
    Do I know God? / Tullian Tchividjian. — 1st ed.
        p. cm.
    Includes bibliographical references (p.) and index.
    1. Assurance (Theology)   2. Salvation—Christianity.   I. Title.
    BT785.T34 2007
    234—dc22

                                2007022647

Printed in the United States of America
2015

10 9 8 7 6

To Mom and Dad

*You were the first to teach me that Christianity
is first and foremost about having a relationship with God.*

Contents

Foreword

The book you now hold in your hand contains the message I have spent more than sixty years of my life proclaiming. From my first book, *Peace with God,* published in 1953, to my most recent book, *The Journey,* I have sought to help people understand how they can truly know God.

As I near the end of my life in this world, it has been my earnest prayer that God would raise up a new generation of voices committed to proclaiming the good news that, in the person of Jesus Christ, God came into this fallen world to rescue sinners from their sin, turning slaves into sons. This book, written by my grandson Tullian Tchividjian, is an answer to my prayer. God has raised up Tullian for such a time as this, to boldly proclaim to the next generation that there is nothing more important than knowing God.

As you will come to find out in these pages, Tullian struggled significantly as a young man before God brought him to this sobering conclusion. Even though Tullian was raised in a loving Christian home, he determined to walk away from all God had given him. After years of searching for satisfaction and certainty apart from God, God answered our prayer by opening Tullian's eyes and helping him to see that only a relationship with God can quench our thirst for contentment.

Almost overnight my wife and I saw a radical change in Tullian. His God-driven pursuit of truth was infectious to us all. He spent the next seven years of his life in college and seminary, studying the Bible, philosophy, our culture, church history, theology, and biblical languages. He has taken the advice of my friend John Stott to be a man of double listening—listening to both the questions of the world and the answers of the Word.

His unique combination of life experience and theological ability makes him a biblically wise counselor for his generation. A dynamic preacher and an accomplished church planter, Tullian here puts his thinking down on paper. He makes his case clearly, compellingly, and—most important—biblically.

My prayer for you, the reader, is that you will listen carefully to what my grandson says here. Apart from the Bible, this may be the most important book you could ever read, because it will help you answer the most important question you could ever ask: Do I know God?

—Billy Graham

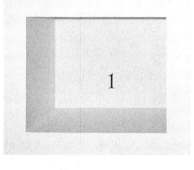

1

The Hope
of Certainty

Is knowing God really possible?

I know whom I have believed,
and I am convinced that he is able to guard
until that Day what has been entrusted to me.
—APOSTLE PAUL (2 TIMOTHY 1:12)

I t was the week after Christmas, and the office was quiet. Most of our staff at New City Church were either out of town or at home with family. I'd taken the week off too, but one morning I stopped by my office to pick up some books. A few minutes after I arrived, someone walked through the front door. His name was Mike. He and his family had been attending New City for a while. Holidays or not, Mike had a question that couldn't wait.

He slumped down in the chair next to the window. He confessed he'd been sitting in the parking lot for more than an hour debating whether he should walk in and talk to me. He had finally mustered the courage to come inside to ask me a single question: "How do I know if I know God?"

As we talked, it became clear that the question had been eating at Mike for at least a year—ever since I'd preached a sermon on Matthew 7. That's the chapter where Jesus warns there will be many who go through life thinking they know God, only to hear chilling words when they meet him in eternity: "I never knew you; depart from me, you workers of lawlessness" (verse 23).

Those eleven words—"I never knew you; depart from me, you workers of lawlessness"—were haunting Mike. He was haunted by the simple, stark tragedy they convey: that a guy can be so badly mistaken about such an important relationship he can go through life thinking he knows God, only to hear a shocker at its end.

"Is it even possible, Tullian, to *know* God?" asked Mike. "I mean, *really* know him?"

Mike took his question further. If knowing God in this life determined whether we received an eternal welcome or its very disturbing opposite, then the stakes were even higher. "How can I *know* that I know God?" he asked.

One look at Mike's face showed me he hadn't driven to my office during Christmas week just to play Stump the Preacher.

Mike was confused and distressed, besieged by doubts. And he wanted answers. No, he *needed* answers.

There's a story behind the story that you should know about Mike, something that might have been pressing him to get at the facts about knowing God. Before Mike started attending New City, he'd never been a churchgoing guy. When he fell ill with cancer, that changed. On his first Sunday at our church, Mike introduced himself and told me about his cancer. He asked me to pray with him and his family, and I did. Today, thankfully, Mike's cancer is in remission. But anyone who's had a brush with death is more likely to think deeply and courageously about life's big questions.

Of course, Mike isn't alone. I meet people almost every day who are struggling with whether God is knowable and, if he is, what it means to have a relationship with him. Recently I received an e-mail from a friend named Curt. Although Curt says he's a Christian, for some time he and his girlfriend had been struggling to integrate their relationships with God into their relationship with each other. They recently broke up. Heartbroken and confused, Curt has been questioning the genuineness of his relationship with God ever since. When he discovered I was writing this book, he wrote:

> Ever since Jill and I broke up, I feel as if I'm slipping away from God, and I need help. When I read your

e-mail about the book you're writing, I almost didn't read it all the way through, but something told me to keep reading. I can't help thinking that God wants me to take my relationship with him a little more seriously. I've been meaning to make an appointment with you, but I've been too full of pride to admit something—I don't really know God as much as I thought I did. I know you're busy, but when things aren't so hectic, I'll be around.

THE HUMAN NEED TO KNOW

The questions Mike and Curt are asking lead me to make an elementary but critical observation: all people throughout history can be divided into two groups—those who know God and those who don't. Simple. True. Potentially devastating.

Fortunately, though, that isn't the end of it. Not by any means. For example, the Bible makes it clear that if you're confused about which group you belong to, you don't have to remain confused. If you do have a relationship with God, he wants you to know it. And if you don't have a relationship with God, he wants you to know it.

The Bible also shows that the flip side of these dramatic statements is true. God does not want you to think you have a relationship with him if you don't. And he doesn't want you to think you do not have a relationship with him if you do.

In this matter, ignorance is not bliss. And thankfully, neither is it necessary.

At our core, you and I have been created to want and need God. In fact, as we'll see in the pages ahead, he designed us specifically to be in a close, life-fulfilling relationship with him. That's why when we're out of relationship to him or we aren't sure where we stand with him, we feel restless, numbed, somehow incomplete. It doesn't matter who we are or how much security we experience in other areas of our lives—as beings created in the image of God, we long for the kind of certainty that only an authentic relationship with God can satisfy.

Do you resonate with this deeply human need for clarity and certainty regarding a relationship with God? If so, then this book is for you. It is my attempt to give Mike, Curt, and every other sincere spiritual seeker credible answers to the all-important question "Do I know God?"

Our Uncertain Generation

Let's admit something right off: most people today are deeply suspicious of the word *certainty*. For one thing, nothing seems certain anymore. Our world is racked by war, social upheaval, natural disasters, recurring pandemics, racial and sectarian hatred, and terrorism. And the list could go on. For another thing, on a more personal level, millions struggle every day with job insecurity, family and marriage breakdowns, financial hardship, and fear.

In a world this unstable, it is hard to believe that we can be certain about anything. Or—if we're honest—that certainty is always desirable.

We all learned about the fanatical religious certainty that drove the terrorists on September 11, 2001. For good reason, we've come to distrust and fear those who operate by any absolute and extreme code, especially a religious one. No wonder our generation is more comfortable with pluralism, tolerance, and the language of statistical probabilities.

It might not be far from the truth to say that doubt is the new absolute. A recent *Time* magazine article suggested that embracing spiritual doubt is the key to defusing the political and cultural tensions between East and West. After all, the writer concluded, spiritual doubt is the only honest position to take: "If God is beyond our categories then God can't be captured for certain."

Is this what you and I are left with then in our quest for certainty with God—spiritual doubt as our only conviction? Given that God is infinite and we are finite, that he is perfect and we are imperfect, is absolute certainty even possible when it comes to knowing God? After all, Isaiah 55:8–9 says:

My thoughts are not your thoughts,

neither are your ways my ways, declares the LORD.

For as the heavens are higher than the earth,

so are my ways higher than your ways

and my thoughts than your thoughts.

My first response to the driving question of this book is a true story. It is the story of a genius who said, "It is not certain that everything is uncertain." His name was Blaise Pascal.

A PHILOSOPHER'S ENCOUNTER WITH FIRE

On August 19, 1662, the French mathematician, physicist, and philosopher Blaise Pascal died at the young age of thirty-nine. Pascal was, according to British scholar Malcolm Muggeridge, "unquestionably one of the greatest intellects Europe ever produced." Following his death, Pascal's servant discovered a piece of parchment sewn carefully into his coat. A cross was inscribed at the top of the parchment, and underneath it were these words, now famously known as the "Memorial":

The year of grace 1654
Monday, 23 November...

. . . .

From about half past ten in the evening until half past
        midnight.

Fire

"God of Abraham, God of Isaac, God of Jacob,"

        [Exodus 3:6] not of philosophers and scholars.

Certainty, certainty, heartfelt, joy, peace.

God of Jesus Christ…

"My God and your God." [John 20:17]

"Thy God shall be my God." [Ruth 1:16]

The world forgotten, and everything except God.

He can only be found by the ways taught in the

        Gospels.

Greatness of the human soul.

"O righteous Father, the world had not known thee,

        but I have known thee." [John 17:25]

Joy, joy, joy, tears of joy,

. . . .

Let me never be cut off from him!

He can only be kept by the ways taught in the

        Gospel.

Sweet and total renunciation.

Total submission to Jesus Christ and my director.

Everlasting joy in return for one day's effort on earth.

"I will not forget thy word." [Psalm 119:16] Amen! [1]

What prompted such an outpouring? On November 23, 1654, Pascal barely escaped being killed when his carriage almost plunged off a bridge. Fifteen days after his brush with death, Pascal experienced a personal encounter with God so powerful, so potent, that he penned those words. For the rest of his life, Pascal kept them near to his heart (literally) so he would never forget his "night of fire"—the night that changed his life forever.

Pascal's near tragedy led him to a joyous experience of God's presence—"Joy, joy, joy, tears of joy.... Let me never be cut off from him!" But what I've always found fascinating about Pascal's "Memorial" is how he tied his experience of joy and peace to certainty. For example, he discovered the certainty of God's supreme value—"The world forgotten, and everything except God." He was certain of God's grace and compassion. He was certain of God's love and favor. He was certain of God's goodness and mercy. He was certain of his future reward as a result of total submission to Christ—"Everlasting joy in return for one day's effort on earth." He knew God, and he *knew* that he knew God—"not of philosophers and scholars," but the living God. And it was this assurance that endowed his life with a wholeness—a greatness of soul—that he had never known before.

Few men in history have thought more deeply about the nature of reality than Pascal. Writes Robert E. Coleman of Gordon-Conwell Theological Seminary, "At an age when others had hardly begun to see the light, [Pascal] had completed the cycle of human knowledge, and seeing its emptiness, directed his remaining energies to knowing him in whom is hidden all the wisdom and the glory of God."[2]

What Pascal discovered on that fiery night was simply this: a man or woman *can* know God. And to *know* that you know God changes everything.

GOD IS NOT SILENT

Of course, most of us aren't genius physicists, philosophers, or mathematicians. Nor have many of us experienced a fiery night with God. So it's only reasonable that we might wonder, *Is certainty with God something that he makes available for ordinary persons who must endure very real limits?*

Again, the Bible's answer is heartening, because we encounter a God who both wants to be known and chooses to reveal himself to all. As the title of a Francis Schaeffer book so memorably put it, *He Is There and He Is Not Silent.* Of course, we can't know everything about God, but what we must know, we can know. As theologian R. C. Sproul wrote:

> The incomprehensibility of God does not mean that we know nothing about God. Rather, it means that our knowledge is partial and limited, falling short of a total or

comprehensive knowledge. The knowledge that God gives of himself through revelation is both real and useful. We can know God to the degree that he chooses to reveal himself.[3]

The first revealing of God is nature itself. Ancient Jews saw the physical world as the garment of God: a shining, sometimes terrifying skin that both covers and partially reveals the Divine Infinite. David the psalmist wrote:

The heavens declare the glory of God,
    and the sky above proclaims his handiwork.
Day to day pours out speech,
    And night to night reveals knowledge. (Psalm 19:1–2)

God's fingerprints are on everything—black holes, nebulas, pink salamanders, ice crystals, a leaf bud unfurling in spring, mold, an atomic particle, a baby's cry, a grandfather's face, you, me. As C. S. Lewis said, "We may ignore, but we can nowhere evade the presence of God. The world is crowded with Him."

Everything in nature points to an exultant, good, and glorious God. Paul described what every pagan in the Roman Empire had already witnessed of this revelation: "What can be known about God is plain to them, because God has shown it to them. For his invisible attributes, namely, his eternal power and divine nature, have been clearly perceived, ever since the creation of the world, in the things that have been made" (Romans 1:19–20).

Since every created thing reveals the Creator in some way, we can say with confidence that God has made himself known—certainly. But the most indispensable and precise revealing of God is in his Word, the Bible.

While God unveils himself generally in nature and in everything good and true, God does so specifically in Scripture. Creation displays the greatness of God; the Bible goes beyond displaying his greatness and reveals how you and I can know this great God. The Bible is God's story. In its pages we learn about God's unfolding plan to restore a broken world. The Bible reveals God "as more than a distant cosmic architect...or an impersonal life force. He is the living God, present and active everywhere."[4]

As we read the Bible, we come to find that the central figure in God's plan, the hero of God's story, is God's own Son, Jesus. According to Hebrews 1:3, "[Jesus] is the radiance of the glory of God and the exact imprint of his nature." He is the Savior sent by God to right all wrongs, mend all that is broken, and reconcile separated, fallen human beings like you and me to God. In nature we learn that we are creatures who depend on a Creator. In Scripture we learn that we are sinners who depend on a Savior (more about this in chapter 2).

In the person of Jesus, we learn something vital about God: he deeply desires to be in relationship with people. He desires this so much, in fact, that he paid the ultimate price so that genuine, unbroken relationship to him could be ours—forever.

THE SURE ANCHORING OF YOUR SOUL

As we explore answers to the question "Do I know God?" we'll first examine what a relationship to God actually means, how we enter into an authentic one, and what we can expect as a result—both now and in our future. Since there is so much confusion today regarding what it means to be spiritual or religious, this book will also identify six ways people deceive themselves into thinking they know God when they do not.

Second, this book will assist as you "examine [yourself], to see whether you are in the faith" (2 Corinthians 13:5) in order to help you "make your calling and election sure" (2 Peter 1:10). The outcome of this rigorous personal inventory for Christians is that we can then confidently enjoy the sure and steadfast anchoring of our soul that true relationship with God promises (Hebrews 6:19).

And finally, this book will suggest practical spiritual disciplines that can help you not only maintain this most significant relationship but flourish emotionally and spiritually in it. I encourage you to use the accompanying study guide either for your personal benefit or in a group of like-minded seekers.

To know your Creator, to know that you are loved, and to

know that you know—that's the simple but profound promise of this book. When you finally understand that truth, your life will be transformed. My earnest prayer for you as you read is that by the last page you will be able to say with passionate certainty in your heart,

Blessed assurance, Jesus is mine!
O what a foretaste of glory divine!
Heir of salvation, purchase of God,
Born of His Spirit, washed in His blood.
This is my story, this is my song.[5]

2

Real Relationship with God

What does it mean to truly know God?

Journeys end in lovers meeting.
—Shakespeare

K*nowing*—the word is so full of human yearning and
promise. Yet especially in the context of the relationships
that matter to us, true knowing remains elusive. And all the more
so when the person we want to know is God.

What does it mean to truly know God? In the last chapter we
saw that God reveals himself, that he wants to be known by us, that
he is knowable—and that we can *know* that we know him. But
before we move further in exploring personal spiritual certainty, we
need to understand what a genuine relationship with God looks

like: how we enter into one if we don't have one; what it means—for us and for God—once we're "related"; and what outcomes we can expect, now and in our future, from knowing God.

Christianity is not just about adhering to a set of doctrines (although it is built on distinctive beliefs), nor is it just about living ethically (although moral choices are encouraged and expected), nor is it just about following a set of religious practices (although taking part in worship services, for example, is important). Christianity is first and foremost about a relationship to God—knowing him truly and personally.

One important distinction surfaces immediately: the difference between knowing *about* God and *knowing* God.

I know many things about the current president of the United States: his likes and dislikes; his views on important issues; details about his family life, background, and so on. Most of this information has come to me through reading, watching news programs, or talking to people who know more about him than I do. I've never met the president or shaken his hand. He doesn't know my name. He doesn't know I exist.

How much would I need to learn about the person who leads our country before I could say truthfully that I really *know* him? before I could say that the two of us have a meaningful personal relationship? In fact, would it even be possible to get from one kind of knowing to the other without an intervening person or event of some kind?

You see the problem. Between knowing about God and knowing God yawns a Grand Canyon of difference. And that difference—call it distance or separateness—is something I understand well from personal experience.

Missing Something

I was blessed to grow up in a loving Christian home, the middle of seven children. I watched my parents live out their faith. As far back as I can remember, I was taught the truth about God. I grew up reading the Bible, praying, going to church, going to Sunday school, and attending Christian schools. I knew virtually every story in the Bible. I could recite the Lord's Prayer, the Ten Commandments, and even the Apostles' Creed. I never doubted that God existed, and I always acknowledged that God sent his Son, Jesus, to die on a cross for sinners like me. I knew this was no fairy tale. My knowledge about God was biblical, orthodox, and impressive.

Sadly, however, while I knew a lot about God, I did not *know* him. As Aunt Anne once told me about being a Christian, "You can have the right stuff in your head but still be missing something." Well, I was missing something, all right—something big!

Here's how that "missing something" played out for me.

It's not an excuse, but I found growing up as a middle child difficult. At times I was bunched with my older siblings, and at other times I was bunched with the younger ones. It seemed like

I ended up bearing the responsibilities of both groups and enjoying the privileges of neither. Coming into adolescence, I wasn't sure who I was or where I fit. Perhaps partly as a result, I rebelled against everything my family stood for, looking instead to other people and places to fill the hole I felt inside.

I didn't rebel halfheartedly either. By the age of sixteen, I had dropped out of high school, managed to get myself kicked out of the house (the police literally escorted me from my parents' property), and set off party hopping across South Florida. At the time, of course, I was very pleased with my achievements. Freed from the constraints of teachers and parents, I pursued pleasure harder than most my age, trying desperately to "find myself" through promiscuity, drugs, and alcohol.

I was on a pleasure–seeking rampage in search of satisfaction and contentment behind every worldly tree and under every worldly rock. I was a man on a hedonistic mission.

But the more I pursued these things, the more lost I felt. The more I drank from the well of worldly bliss, the thirstier I became; the faster I ran toward godless pleasure, the further I felt from true fulfillment. Pretty much everything about the real me was broken, foolish, and crusted over with self and sin. By the time I reached my early twenties, I was even more confused about who I was and where I fit than I had been as a teenager. I felt like I was stumbling through life blindfolded, without direction or understanding. Life made no sense. I decided there had to be more to who I was than what I was experiencing.

I couldn't understand why my master plan wasn't working. What had I done wrong? Where had I miscalculated?

I hadn't taken into account the amazing grace of God! I radically underestimated the determination of Divine love and mercy. In everything I was doing, I started to feel, in the words of C. S. Lewis, "the unrelenting approach of Him who I desperately desired not to meet." The Hound of Heaven was on my tail, and my persistent attempts to outrun him were proving to be futile.

I cried out to God for pardon and help, believing he was the only one who could deliver me. God answered and helped me see that my hunger for identity could be satisfied only in something that I'd never asked for when I was growing up, that I hadn't inherited from my godly parents, and that I'd certainly never found in my headlong, self-centered pursuits: a relationship with God himself.

What happened? I experienced "a magnificent defeat" at the hand of God. God rescued me, and for the first time in more than twenty years, I rested. God accomplished what I couldn't. He moved me from one side of the Grand Canyon to the other. I was literally "a new creation" (2 Corinthians 5:17). I knew God!

The point is, if you really want to know God, you have to enter into a personal relationship with him. And that's what I want to talk about in the rest of this chapter. I want to talk about what separates us from God, what brings us to God, and what kind of bond we experience once we're in genuine relationship to God.

So Close, Yet So Far

You and I were created by God to know him, plain and simple. Every single human being was designed—hard-wired—specifically to be in relationship to God. But something's wrong, and all of us know it. If we were honest, we would admit that deep down we sense something necessary is missing. We sense a homesickness we can't explain. The truth is, only when the distance between us and God is bridged can we experience the fullness, the homecoming—and the certainty—we earnestly seek. As Saint Augustine prayed, "You have created us for Yourself, O God, and our hearts are restless until they find their rest in You."

What keeps us apart and restless? An uncrossable chasm of separation. The Bible word for it is *sin.*

In our narcissistic culture the word *sin* is not popular. But actually it's a pointed, practical word. Sin, says J. I. Packer, is "a universal deformity of human nature, found at every point in every person.… It is a rebellious reaction to God's call and command, a spirit of fighting God in order to play God."[1] None of us, in other words, is sin free. As Paul wrote, "All have sinned and fall short of the glory of God" (Romans 3:23).

None is righteous, no, not one;
> no one understands;
> no one seeks for God.

All have turned aside. (Romans 3:10–12)

Our own sin nature and sinful acts preclude an intimate relationship with a holy God. (It only makes sense—selfishness and betrayal fracture human relationships too.) The sin virus warps how we understand ourselves and God, blights how we treat others, skews what we want (even if it's killing us), and drastically limits what we can do to change. The fact is, we cannot get over the canyon of sin without help. God must act.

And God has acted. On our behalf, he crossed over the canyon to rescue sinners. The Bible word for this astonishing gift of mercy and life is *salvation.*

Salvation, like *sin,* is an eminently practical word—although a much happier one. Salvation is what a baby girl playing in the middle of the freeway needs; she doesn't understand the danger she's in, and she couldn't escape it if she did. Salvation is what the hardened murderer on death row needs; he's about to receive society's just judgment for his actions, and if pardon and freedom are to come, they must come from outside his cell, from someone who holds the power of pardon and release. Both the baby and the criminal need rescuing. They can neither earn nor fabricate their salvation; their only hope is to receive it as a gift.

You and I are born estranged from God. We live in self-centered rebellion, stubbornly choosing to be "God" for ourselves. And we justly deserve the true God's judgment. What we all need—desperately—is to be saved.

The good news of the gospel is simply this: in the midst of our hopeless and helpless circumstance, God sent his Son, Jesus Christ, to save sinners like you and me. God's costly gift, however, requires our humble response of acknowledging our need of him and receiving in faith the salvation God offers. The Bible promises, "If you confess with your mouth that Jesus is Lord and believe in your heart that God raised him from the dead, you will be saved" (Romans 10:9).

In Christ, God promises to make us new creatures (2 Corinthians 5:17). We gain a new beginning, a new family, a new purpose, a new power, and a new destiny. And best of all for our discussion in this book, we gain a new relationship with God that is real, absolutely certain, and eternal. This relationship has little in common with the "knowing about" variety. Rather, we enter into the genuine "knowing" fellowship of a loving Father.

The many dimensions of salvation are described in the Bible with some big words—for example, *justification, sanctification, glorification,* and *redemption.* But the relational dimension, which is our topic here, is captured in a simple but emotionally charged family word: *adoption.*

ORPHANS THEN; NOW SONS, NOW DAUGHTERS

When you and I turn from our sins and enter into real relationship with God, we receive a completely new identity. We who were once lost sinners, spiritual orphans, slaves to our own humanity, are now adopted into God's family. And we are given the privilege of calling him Father. *Father?* Yes!

Let me show you from the Bible what I mean.

In Galatians 4:4–6 Paul wrote that God the Father sent Jesus to buy back sinners from their enslavement "so that we might receive *adoption* as sons" (verse 5, emphasis added). Paul used the term *huiothesia,* which means "the process or act of being adopted." In fact, Paul used the same word five times in three of his letters. He really wanted to drive his point home.

And Paul's point is this: because of sin, we're all born alienated from God. That is, we come into this world as spiritual orphans, relationally disconnected from our Creator. But God, because of his amazing grace, chooses to adopt sinners into his family. He chooses to turn slaves into sons. Before God created the world, he already chose to adopt spiritually orphaned, undeserving sinners into his eternal family as fully alive sons and daughters (Ephesians 1:4–5).

Interestingly, according to the Bible, each person of the

Godhead—Father, Son, and Holy Spirit—works to make our adoption happen.

- God the Father *appoints* the adoption of individual sinners: "When the Gentiles heard this, they began rejoicing and glorifying the word of the Lord, and as many as were appointed to eternal life believed" (Acts 13:48).

- God the Son *accomplishes* adoption for individual sinners: "The Son of Man came not to be served but to serve, and to give his life as a ransom for many" (Matthew 20:28).

- God the Spirit *applies* adoption to individual sinners: "In him you also, when you heard the word of truth, the gospel of your salvation, and believed in him, were sealed with the promised Holy Spirit, who is the guarantee of our inheritance until we acquire possession of it, to the praise of his glory" (Ephesians 1:13–14).

So, as Packer says, a Christian is "one who has God as Father." Christians are people who have cried out to God in faith and received "the Spirit of adoption as sons, by whom we cry, 'Abba! Father!'" (Romans 8:15). Knowing God is nothing less than being able to call the Creator of this universe "Daddy."

And that's a whole lot different from simply knowing facts about God.

Mornings When She Runs In

My little girl, Genna, calls me "Daddy." I love those mornings when she runs into my room, jumps into my bed, and says, "Good morning, Daddy!" She knows, with complete confidence, how much I love to embrace her and how I will always welcome her with open arms. It's that picture of a confident child running into the arms of a loving father that the Bible compares to God's relationship with his own adopted children.

I also love the word *adoption*. It describes perfectly what our relationship to God really means. Adoption isn't simply a concept or a big theological word; it's a family word, a loving parent-child word. It promises belonging, closeness, and a brand-new and highly favored identity. And it says much about the heart of a loving, determined, all-powerful Father who goes looking for children who will forever bear his name.

Parents who adopt often say they've found new insight into God's heart. That's true for Christian singer Steven Curtis Chapman and his wife, Mary Beth, who adopted a baby girl from China in 2000.

When Mary Beth first held baby Shaohannah, she experienced one of those moments she knew could only come from God. "I was holding this little person and at that moment I would have died for her," she wrote. "It was so emotional. It was really the first time, other than committing my life to the Lord, that I just looked up and went, 'Okay, I get it, I get it. I know what you did for me.' "

And Steven reported, "Until we adopted Shaohannah, I didn't fully understand the depth of what Jesus has done for us. [Without Christ] I was hopeless, without a future, without a name…then Jesus came into my life, gave me hope and a future. He gave me a new name. Adoption is the perfect picture of what God has done for each of us in making us his children through Christ."[2]

A RELATIONSHIP WE CAN BOTH KNOW AND FEEL

I have a journalist friend who used to travel in the third world reporting for Christian development organizations. His travels often took him through Christian-run orphanages.

"Those kids are starved for so much," he says. "But I think there are two things they want most. They want to know they're loved, without any doubts or games, and they want to know that someday someone will adopt them into a loving family that no one can ever take away."

As spiritual orphans, you and I want the same things. Thankfully, when we place our faith in Jesus Christ and God adopts us into his family, two of the most foundational things he wants us to know about our new relationship are (1) that our relationship in God's family is secure forever and (2) that we can expect to experience that security internally. Bible teachers call these two foundational truths *eternal security* and *assurance of salvation.* Since these two ideas are so often misunderstood, I want to make sure you are clear about them before we proceed.

Eternal Security

Eternal security means that once God adopts you into his family, your relationship to him is permanent and forever. Nothing and no one can take it away. As Paul wrote in Romans, "Neither death nor life, nor angels nor rulers, nor things present nor things to come, nor powers, nor height nor depth, nor anything else in all creation, will be able to separate us from the love of God in Christ Jesus our Lord" (Romans 8:38–39). God will never disown you.

On the same subject, Jesus said, "My sheep hear my voice, and I know them, and they follow me. I give them eternal life, and they will never perish, and no one will snatch them out of my hand. My Father, who has given them to me, is greater than all, and no one is able to snatch them out of the Father's hand" (John 10:27–29). God holds his adopted children in his hand, and he promises to never let them go.

Once God adopts you into his family, then no matter how badly you behave or how terribly you fail, God will never disinherit you. You are his forever. He will always be your Father, and you will always be his adopted child. No matter what. It's true that disobedience can disrupt your *fellowship* with God, but you cannot lose your *relationship* to God as your Father (more on this in chapter 8).

When I rebelled at the age of sixteen and my mom and dad had to kick me out of the house, they didn't stop being my mom and dad. My brothers and sisters remained my brothers and sisters. I still carried the family name. My relationship to the family did not change, but my fellowship with them did. My rebellion couldn't change my relationship to my family, because relationship depends on birth. But my rebellion did sever my fellowship with them, because fellowship depends on behavior.

Eternal security, then, is an external, objective fact. It is something God does for us, and we can't undo it.

Assurance of Salvation

Assurance of salvation describes the internal, subjective nature of our relationship to God. We experience assurance when we are internally aware of our eternal security. Assurance is our sense of security. When God adopts you into his family, he not only wants you to be *externally* secure, but he also wants you to feel *internally* secure.

In plain language, that means if you're a Christian, God wants you to experience—deep inside—the reality that you are no longer a slave to sin but are now his adopted child. He wants you to know that he loves you! He wants you to know that he has saved you from the penalty of sin, that he is now saving you from the power of sin, and that one day he will save you from the presence of sin altogether. He doesn't just want you to be forgiven; he also wants you to *feel* forgiven. He wants you to enjoy the still waters and green pastures that friendship with God offers. He wants you to go through life confidently knowing that you are his forever and that there is no need to fear ultimate judgment.

Even though God doesn't want his children to doubt their relationship to him, most Christians experience seasons of relational doubt (more about this in chapter 10). The Bible makes it clear that it's possible to be in a relationship with God but lose the inner awareness of that relationship. In other words, it's possible to *be* relationally secure without *feeling* relationally secure. As we'll see, there are many reasons why God might let his children experience a season of doubt, but he never wants this doubt to be continuous. He wants his children to know on the inside that they are his children. John Stott said, "Clearly one cannot enjoy a gift unless one knows that one possesses it. Therefore, if God means us to receive and enjoy eternal life, he must mean us to know we possess it."[3]

Knowing you are a child of God changes the way you live here and now. Assurance of salvation produces a life that joyfully accepts hard struggles and suffering, knowing that the best is yet to come. In the face of ongoing opposition, nothing can enable you to keep on keeping on like the internal assurance that you are a child of God. It was that assurance that led the persecuted children of God mentioned in Hebrews 10:34 to joyfully accept the plundering of their property "since [they] *knew* that [they]…had a better possession and an abiding one" (emphasis added).

Truly knowing and feeling your relationship to God equip you with the peace you need to walk through this life confidently and to bear the burdens that pile on you every day. "Assurance is no less than heaven let down into the soul," said one seventeenth-century bishop, and he was right. To *know* that you know God is truly a taste of heaven on earth.

My granddad once said, "I would not change places with the wealthiest and most influential person in the world. I would rather be a child of the King, a joint-heir with Christ, a member of the Royal Family in heaven. I know where I've come from, I know why I'm here, I know where I'm going—and I have peace in my heart. His peace floods my heart and overwhelms my soul!"[4]

Remembering a Time and Place

It's important to mention before the end of this chapter that while many Christians can remember a time, a place, even a moment when their relationship to God began, many others can't.

I grew up in a church that pressured people to identify a particular time and place when they became Christians, when they were adopted into God's family. In fact, I grew up believing that if I could not recall the moment God saved me, then I was at best a second-class Christian or at worst not a Christian at all.

I really wrestled with this about six years ago. My mom told me that I prayed and asked Jesus to come into my life when I was five years old, but I don't remember anything about it. What I do remember is how drastically my life changed when I was twenty-one.

It frustrated me not knowing for sure whether my relationship with God began when I was five and "prayed the prayer" or when I was twenty-one and my life clearly changed. Did I become a Christian when I was five and then simply rebelled until I was twenty-one, at which point I rededicated my life to God? Or did I become a Christian for the first time at twenty-one? I didn't know, and it really bothered me. I wanted to pinpoint the time and place. My spiritual life depended on it, or so I thought.

About that time I had lunch with Arnie, one of my wisest, most godly friends. As I shared my struggle with him, he looked at me and said, "Tullian, does it really matter? The Bible has a lot more to say about how the Christian life ends than how it begins."

I dropped my fork. He was right. I thought about all those places in the Bible that speak about finishing the race, obtaining the prize, pressing on, and straining forward. I felt a huge weight lift off my shoulders. Pinpointing the time and place I became a

Christian didn't matter. What did matter was my daily pursuit of God. What did matter was my need to continue in the faith from that day forward.

John Stott said, "He who stands firm in the faith to the end will be saved, not because salvation is the reward of endurance, but because endurance is the hallmark of the saved." Arnie helped me see that my ongoing endurance, not my ability to isolate a moment when my relationship with God began, is what helps me be certain about my relationship with God.

The truth is, there are different types of testimonies. Everybody's story of how God saved them is unique. True, salvation happens in an instant, a single moment in time. But some people are able to remember that moment, and others aren't. That's okay. What really matters is that all of us can know we are God's children, adopted into his family, if we are currently pressing on in the faith.

If you're not sure yet whether you've been adopted by God, know this: God promises that if you call on his name, he will hear. Don't make the mistake of thinking that you must "get yourself right" before you cry out for salvation, for as an old hymn puts it:

> Let not conscience make you linger,
> Nor of fitness fondly dream;

All the fitness He requireth
Is to feel your need of Him.[5]

When you feel your desperation for God and call out to him for rescue, that's all you need to receive the free gift of pardon, new life, and lasting relationship that only God can give.

3

Avoiding the Many

How can I be sure that I am not deceived
by the false certainty the Bible warns about?

The day of judgment will reveal strange things.
The hopes of many,
who were thought great Christians while they lived,
will be utterly confounded.

—J. C. RYLE

Now that we have a clearer understanding of what it means
to know God, we're ready to reengage with the troubling
questions from Mike and Curt that launched this exploration:

- What if I think I know God but really don't?
- What can I do now to make sure I never hear God say,
  "I never knew you; depart from me"?

In the last chapter we explored the beautiful truth that if God has adopted you into his family, he wants you to be aware of your saving relationship to him as your heavenly Father. He wants you to have a true sense of your security. Knowing that you know God gives you the lasting courage, strength, and comfort you need to endure the wilderness of life in this broken world (Hebrews 10:34).

But the Bible is clear that you can also experience *false* assurance—that is, you can think you're a Christian when you really aren't. As we'll see in more detail in the next three chapters, not all who think they have a relationship with God actually do. In fact, if we look again at the verses that came back to haunt Mike, we see Jesus predicting that a number of his followers will step into eternity holding on to a mistaken notion of where they stand with God. Here is a fuller text of his remarks:

> Not everyone who says to me, "Lord, Lord," will enter the kingdom of heaven, but the one who does the will of my Father who is in heaven. On that day many will say to me, "Lord, Lord, did we not prophesy in your name, and cast out demons in your name, and do many mighty works in your name?" And then will I declare to them, "I never knew you; depart from me, you workers of lawlessness." (Matthew 7:21–23)

I wouldn't say that Jesus was describing spiritual dabblers here. Would you? These followers have called him Lord, have accomplished remarkable feats in his name, and yet enter eternity shocked to discover that they remain strangers to God.

Notice something else. Jesus didn't say "some" would find themselves in this position. He didn't say there would be "quite a few" or even "more than you would expect." No, Jesus said "many."

Many people who sincerely think they know God will one day hear the chilling words "I never knew you; depart from me, you workers of lawlessness." C. S. Lewis described this horrific experience as being "banished from the presence of him who is everywhere and erased from the knowledge of him who knows all."

Given the dire consequences of making wrong assumptions in this matter, we should proceed thoughtfully and humbly. "If a person is wrong about being right with God," says Donald Whitney, "[then] ultimately it really doesn't matter what else he or she is right about."[1] So we're not being alarmists to care greatly about getting it right.

DISAPPOINTMENT WITH GOD'S PEOPLE

Surely you've noticed that many people who call themselves Christians behave in un-Christian ways. In an interview with the *Washington Post,* Dr. Timothy Larsen, professor of theology at Wheaton

College in Illinois, said that in a sense atheism is "a disappoint-ment with God which flows from a disappointment with his people, the church." Os Guinness, a Christian social scientist, pointed this out in a lecture he recently gave at Louisiana State University on the topic of hypocrisy. The title of his message was "The One Unanswerable Objection to the Christian Faith: Chris-tians." In his talk he quoted George Bernard Shaw who once said, "Christianity might actually be a good thing if anyone ever tried it." This failure of those who profess Christ to follow their leader undoubtedly inspired a bumper sticker I saw the other day. It read, "Dear Jesus, please save me from your followers."

To be sure, the charge of hypocrisy leveled at Christians too often serves as an excuse to ignore and refuse the rightful claims God makes on our lives. When it comes to Christianity, many are guilty of what logicians call "the genetic fallacy." That is, refusing to believe in God because of the shortcomings of his followers. God's existence and ones relationship to God has to be evaluated on its own terms regardless of how many "Christian hypocrites" there may be. As Guinness pointed out, "The decisive question is not whether believers fall short of their beliefs but whether those beliefs are true." Even the existentialist philosopher Albert Camus, who was no friend of Christianity, noted that "beliefs should be judged by their peaks, not their by-products." Never-theless, it does often seem like there's a sad disconnect between Christ and many who claim to follow him. Is it possible that many such professing followers of Christ in reality do not know him? that they (or we) could be numbered among the "many" Christ warned about?

Newsweek magazine published some startling statistics concerning what Americans believe about Jesus Christ: 78 percent of Americans believe Jesus rose from dead; 75 percent say he was sent to earth to forgive mankind of sin; 81 percent say they are Christians. The magazine went on to report that Christianity is now the world's largest religion, with two billion professing believers (roughly one third of the earth's population).

Now, I'm in no position to determine who knows God and who doesn't. But it seems to me that if 81 percent of Americans truly have a relationship with God through Jesus Christ, this country would look a lot different than it does, indicating that many who think they know God, actually do not.

The hope I hold out to you is this: It's not necessary to remain self-deluded about one's position with God. It's not too late to understand the true basis for receiving God's welcome into eternity. It's not too late to come to know God.

But in order to be shaken out of dangerous complacency and be shorn of false assurance, you need to know that your abilities and accomplishments, even if they're performed in Christ's name, are not what God is looking for. And sadly, this self-delusion can persist even in those who outwardly seem closest to the Lord. I'll give you an example.

THOSE WHO SEEM MOST GODLY MAY NOT BE

One day Jesus "called the twelve and began to send them out two by two" on a mission among the towns and villages of Israel (Mark 6:7). This outreach would spread his message, teach the disciples about the power of God working through them, and prepare the future apostles for their missionary work around the known world. "So they went out and proclaimed that people should repent. And they cast out many demons and anointed with oil many who were sick and healed them" (verses 12–13).

Note something here: all twelve disciples were included, Judas Iscariot among them. The same Judas Iscariot who would later trade his Master for a purse of coins. Judas, then, was evidently one of those who preached repentance, cast out demons, and healed the sick. And for all we know, he may have done much more of merit during his three years or so traveling about the countryside with the Lord.

Judas certainly had reason to protest, "Lord, Lord, did I not prophesy in your name, and cast out demons in your name, and do many mighty works in your name?" when he appeared before God following his suicidal death. But what became of him then? We have a plain enough clue from out of Jesus's own mouth. "Woe to that man by whom the Son of Man is betrayed!" said the Son of Man. "It would have been better for that man if he had not been born" (Mark 14:21).

Even one of the twelve heard the order to depart from God's presence.

And so we'd better ask ourselves, what about us?

Preaching sermons that turn people toward Jesus, singing gospel songs that move listeners' hearts, offering counsel that guides the confused, raising church buildings with one's own money and labor, feeding the hungry at a skid row rescue mission, even writing a book about knowing God (I remind myself)— none of this, or anything like it, qualifies a person to become a child of God.

FINDING FREEDOM FROM FALSE ASSURANCE

In this chapter and the following two, we'll explore the possibility of possessing false assurance about our relationship to God.

Throughout history, people have been fascinated by Jesus— who he was, what he did, and how he taught. But fascination with Jesus doesn't necessarily mean one has a relationship with him. As a pastor, I talk to people all the time who confuse having knowledge *about* God with truly *knowing* God. They may believe many true things about God, but in many cases there's no real evidence they know him—and the consequences are disastrous.

I want to be extremely careful in these pages not to pass personal judgment on the spiritual state of others. The fact is, no one—theologian, pastor, or otherwise—can or should do that.

"Man looks on the outward appearance, but the Lord looks on the heart" (1 Samuel 16:7). Our primary mission in these pages is to follow the biblical injunction to examine our own relationship—or lack of it—with God so we can invite the truth to change us as needed and so we can enjoy the peace and strength he promises for those who know him.

As I said earlier in this book, God doesn't want you to think you have a relationship with him if you really don't. So how can you avoid this kind of false assurance? How can you know that you possess true relationship with God?

In the rest of this chapter, I want to identify two ways you might be deceived into thinking you have a relationship with God when you really don't.

DECEPTION 1: "I PRAYED THE SINNER'S PRAYER. ISN'T THAT ENOUGH?"

I met Jason four years ago when his girlfriend, Krista, asked me to talk to him about his relationship with God. Krista had started attending the church where I preached, but Jason refused to join her. They were unmarried and living together and moving in opposite spiritual directions. But Krista thought maybe I could help.

Jason agreed to meet with me. I soon learned that he had prayed the sinner's prayer at a Christian youth conference when he was in high school. Apparently one evening the speaker delivered a powerful message about heaven and hell that scared Jason down the aisle. When he reached the front of the auditorium, with tears streaming down his face, the speaker asked everyone who had come forward to "repeat this prayer after me." Jason repeated the prayer word for word. When it was over, the speaker declared, "If you just prayed that prayer, you are now a child of God. Heaven is your true home, and you never need to fear hell again. Welcome to the family of God!"

That assurance put Jason at ease. From that moment forward, he rarely thought about heaven or hell again. He hung on to that speaker's promise, believing he was eternally secure in the family of God.

As the years went on, however, nothing about Jason changed. He continued in sin without thinking twice about it, because that speaker had assured him that since he had walked the aisle and prayed the prayer, he was a child of God from that moment forward, regardless of the way he lived.

As Jason and I talked, it was clear to me that he did not know God. He possessed some factual knowledge about God, but he did not *know* God. He did not have an authentic, eternal relationship with Jesus Christ. Regardless of what the speaker led Jason to believe at the youth conference, he was spiritually lost, still dead in his trespasses and sins (Ephesians 2:1), still without a saving relationship with his Creator.

I never saw Jason again.

What he and others like him fail to understand is that entering into a relationship with God is a spiritual transaction, not a physical one. In other words, God doesn't save and adopt you into his eternal family just because you once repeated the words of a prayer, walked an aisle, raised your hand in church, or signed a commitment card.

You enter into a spiritual relationship with God when he opens your blind eyes and softens your hard heart and you become aware for the first time that you are a great sinner and Christ is a great Savior. At that point you run to him because you understand you need him and you want him.

In other words, we enter into a relationship with God when we respond to God's initiative, not when God responds to ours. We love him because he first loved us. In fact, his love for us *caused* our love for him.

> Long my imprisoned spirit lay,
> Fast bound in sin and nature's night;
> Thine eye diffused a quickening ray;
> I woke, the dungeon flamed with light;
> My chains fell off, my heart was free,
> I rose, went forth, and followed Thee.[2]

Don't get me wrong—praying the sinner's prayer or walking forward at a Billy Graham crusade or raising your hand in church isn't wrong or inappropriate in itself. But it can mislead you into thinking that such an action alone offers you a guarantee of salvation and entry into God's family. It doesn't.

Physical, external acts like repeating the words of a prayer don't turn slaves into sons. Divinely crafted internal revolutions do. And initially, only God knows who those people are, because it is an act of God—not an act of man—that brings people into an eternal relationship with him.

A Caution for Pastors

As a pastor, I feel the need to caution my peers who might unwittingly lead people into thinking they have a relationship with God just because they repeated a prayer or raised their hands at an invitation.

Not long ago I listened to someone preach a powerful message about the good news that God saves all who confess their sins and turn to Jesus Christ. When he concluded, he implored those who did not have a relationship with God to respond by repeating a prayer after him. After leading his listeners in a simple and straightforward prayer, he confidently declared that everyone who had just repeated his prayer was now a child of God.

I winced. But not because I thought God hadn't saved anyone who prayed that prayer. On the contrary, I believe with all my heart that those who honestly confessed their need for God that day began a relationship with him that will last forever. Rather, I winced because the preacher based his promise that God had saved them on an external ritual rather than an internal reality.

That preacher couldn't possibly know that all those who repeated his prayer had genuinely surrendered their lives to God. So there was no way he should have guaranteed that everyone who prayed his prayer became a child of God that day.

My granddad, Billy Graham, has preached the gospel of Jesus Christ to more people than anyone in history. His message is simple: God came into this world in the person of Jesus Christ to rescue sinners from their slavery to sin and to make them new creatures. His preaching has always been clear and passionate.

At the conclusion of every sermon, he invites people to enter into relationship with God through Christ and calls them to get out of their seats and make their way to the front of the auditorium or stadium. Then he leads them in a prayer. His typical prayer goes something like this: "O God, I'm a sinner. I'm sorry for my sin. I'm willing to turn from my sin and turn to Christ. I confess Jesus as Savior and Lord. I want to follow him and serve him for the rest of my life. In Jesus's name, amen."

My granddad would be the first to tell you that not everyone who goes forward and prays that prayer becomes a child of God. No one but God knows who truly surrenders his or her life to him. So instead of saying, "If you just prayed that prayer, you are now a child of God," my granddad says, "If you just prayed that prayer, we have counselors on hand who would like to talk with you, and we also have some literature we would like to give you." He chooses his words carefully, because he does not want people to think they are assured of their salvation simply because they came forward and prayed the prayer. He knows there is nothing magical about raising hands, walking forward, or repeating prayers. He knows that becoming a child of God is a spiritual transaction between God and the individual, a transaction initially invisible to the human eye.

Preachers and spiritual counselors potentially deceive people when they assure them that they're saved based on an external act. In this way, even with the best intentions, they contribute to the problem of many people who, like Jason, believe they are right with God when they aren't. It reminds me of Jeremiah 6:14, where God strongly warns those who proclaim "Peace, peace" when there is no peace.

Don't misunderstand me. I'm not saying that preachers and spiritual counselors should quit pleading with people to respond to the good news that God saves sinners. Paul himself said, "We are ambassadors for Christ, God making his appeal through us. We implore you on behalf of Christ, be reconciled to God" (2 Corinthians 5:20). God clearly expects Christians to deliver his saving message to the world. "How are they to call on him in whom they have not believed? And how are they to believe in him of whom they have never heard? And how are they to hear without someone preaching?... 'How beautiful are the feet of those who preach the good news!' " (Romans 10:14–15).

But God alone saves sinners. God alone softens hard hearts and opens blind eyes. So we dare not assure people they are adopted into God's family based on a physical, external act. There is no prayer we can lead or response we can plead for that can guarantee someone's relationship with God.

DECEPTION 2: "I REMEMBER THE TIME I MADE A DECISION FOR CHRIST. ISN'T THAT ENOUGH?"

A lot of people think they have a relationship with God because they can remember a time when they decided to follow Jesus. Perhaps, like Jason, you remember a youth conference or a church service when you walked forward. Or maybe you remember a conversation with a Christian friend or one of your parents in which you invited Jesus into your heart. And you've been told that as long as you can recall that event, you can know for certain your relationship with God is genuine. Regardless of what your life has looked like from that moment until now, if you can remember a time when you made a choice for Jesus, you can know you are eternally saved.

Theologians have a name for this erroneous view: *decisional regeneration.* But the Bible never says that simply remembering a time in your life when you made a decision for Christ guarantees you a relationship with God—never!

What the Bible does say is that if you really want to be certain about your relationship with God, then you should examine yourself to see whether you are in the faith (2 Corinthians 13:5). In other words, if you want to know that you know God, if you want to experience that assurance in your heart, then you should look for evidence in what you love and how you live (more on this in chapters 7 and 8).

A few weeks ago a woman approached me after church and asked me to pray for her son. He was in his thirties and on his way back to prison. Everything she told me about him led me to believe that he didn't know God. So as I prayed, I asked God to save her son, to make her son a Christian. Halfway through my prayer, however, she interrupted me and said her son *was* a Christian and I didn't need to pray for his salvation. That confused me, so I asked her how she knew he was a Christian. She said she remembered that one night a few years ago her son had walked forward after a church service. As in the case of Jason, his life showed no evidence that he had changed. But because his mom could remember that event, she was convinced he knew God.

To be sure, remembering God's activity in our past is beautiful and important. My point is this: we can't assume that our relationship with God is real if our only basis for that assumption is a past event, whatever it might have been. Instead, we need to ask ourselves, *How am I living?* and *What am I loving?* None of us enters into a relationship with God merely by raising a hand, praying a sinner's prayer, walking an aisle, or remembering a decision made years ago, especially if our lives show no evidence that our prayer or decision made any difference.

The Paths of Religion and Spirituality

But what about people who go to church regularly? What about people who teach Sunday school or tithe or sit on church boards or even preach sermons? They've been religious—isn't that enough?

And what about people who are serious about spirituality? They have found some kind of spiritual fulfillment—isn't *that* enough?

We'll look at these two common kinds of false assurance in the next chapter.

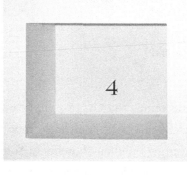

4

The Promise
of Proximity

Does being sincerely religious or spiritual
mean I know God?

The world is...a kind of spiritual kindergarten
where millions of bewildered infants
are trying to spell "God" with the wrong blocks.
—EDWIN ARLINGTON ROBINSON

Howard is a deeply religious man. His parents had him baptized when he was an infant, and he's served his church for more than seventy-five years. He spent his career teaching biology in several prestigious Midwest universities, but he spent his free time and 10 percent of his income on his church—and he still does.

Howard works on his church's mission board and every year accompanies the church's boys' choir to Europe. He also spends two weeks every spring building churches in South America. He never misses a worship service, even when he visits his children in Southern California. In fact, he's as committed to the church he attends in Southern California as he is to his Midwestern home church. He works in church-run soup kitchens, helps out directing traffic before services, and volunteers wherever he sees a need.

Howard loves his church. But God? Ironically, Howard is not so certain. "I don't know. I don't really think about it that much," he admits. "Yeah, I'm pretty sure God exists, but I'm not really all that sure who—or what—God is. Maybe when I die, that's it; it's all over. I don't know. But when I die, if I find out there really is a God waiting for me, I can say I lived a pretty good life and I served his church. I can't even imagine what my life would be like if I didn't have my church."

Many people today, like Howard, think that if they're religious, they're relationally right with God—right enough at least to be welcomed by him into heaven (should God and heaven exist). Still others think that if they're spiritual—if they pursue and practice a receptiveness to God's presence as best they understand it—they must be relationally connected to God. So in this chapter I want to look at two additional ways—religious behavior and spiritual sensitivity—by which people might conclude they have achieved an eternal relationship with God when in fact they haven't.

For the purposes of our discussion here, I will use the word *religious* to identify one's external devotions and the word *spiritual* to identify one's internal devotions. Of course, a true relationship with God involves both external and internal devotion. Authentic Christianity is both religious and spiritual. But as we'll see, it's possible for someone to be profoundly religious and/or deeply spiritual without ever knowing God.

DECEPTION 3: "I'M RELIGIOUS. ISN'T THAT ENOUGH?"

As we saw in Jesus's remarks in Matthew 7:21–23, it's possible—in fact, easy—to do much good in the name of God without having real affection or love for God or a personal relationship with him. Unfortunately, I think that describes my friend Howard.

The Bible describes many deeply religious people who didn't really know God. Probably the clearest example is the Pharisees.

An Ancient Problem

During Jesus's day, the Pharisees were a large, well-respected, rigorously devout religious group within Judaism. They were particularly influential in Galilee, where Jesus conducted much of his early ministry.

No one doubted the Pharisees' religious commitment. They organized every part of their lives around God's Law as it had been revealed through Moses in the Pentateuch (the first five books of the Bible). They were so serious about their religion, in fact, that they created an immense body of secondary rules for how the Mosaic Law should be understood and applied. For example, the Jewish Talmud, a collection of oral rabbinic teachings, lists thirty-nine categories of work that were prohibited on the Sabbath. Each of these categories was further subdivided into thirty-nine sections, creating more than fifteen hundred rules and regulations that the Pharisees tried to obey for the sake of the Sabbath.

No detail of life seemed to escape their religious scrutiny. Here's a sampling of their Sabbath rules: "It was forbidden to unfasten a button, cut your toenails, or carry anything heavier than a dried fig. A man could not wear false teeth, because if they fell out, he would have to carry them, and that would be work. A tailor could not carry a needle in his pocket on the Sabbath because that was one of the tools of his trade, so carrying it would be work."[1]

Without question, the Pharisees were dedicated, religious people. Yet Jesus reserved his harshest criticisms for them. Why? Because Jesus saw that while on the outside they were religiously devout, inside they were relationally devoid. (He called them "whitewashed tombs" [Matthew 23:27]) He knew they were obsessed with practicing their religion but careless about knowing the God of their religion. They were devoted to the religious letter of the Law (dos and don'ts) but not the relational spirit of the Law (captured in Jesus's commands to love the Lord your God with all your heart, mind, and strength and to love your neighbor as yourself).

Rebuking the Pharisees for their arrogant double standards, Jesus said,

> You hypocrites! Well did Isaiah prophesy of you when he said:
>
> "This people honors me with their lips,
>   but their heart is far from me;
> in vain do they worship me." (Matthew 15:7–9)

It's easy to be hard on the Pharisees, but have you noticed how easy it is for church activities—especially when we deeply invest our time, energy, and money—to give us the feeling that we're on intimate terms with God? Many pastors I talk to see how deluded we can become. The truth is, rather than guaranteeing a relationship to God, religious activity can actually hinder us from knowing him. We can easily fall into the trap of thinking that religious achievements are all he wants.

But God wants so much more. He isn't primarily interested in our religious activities. Rather, he wants us to know, love, and serve *him*. As an old hymn states, "Love so amazing, so divine, demands my soul, my life, my all."[2]

A Contemporary Problem

My friend Steve recently told me a story about his childhood pastor. He was a devoutly religious man. He had served the same church for more than twenty years. One morning he was preaching a sermon about the cross of Christ and the salvation God had secured for his children. In the middle of his sermon, the pastor broke down and wept, then bowed his head and prayed out loud, asking God to save him. He became a Christian through listening to himself preach! Here was a man who had ministered in God's church for years but who suddenly realized he did not know God.

My grandfather says that when he invites people to enter into a relationship with God through Christ at the end of his messages, many pastors and church leaders often come forward. They, too, finally recognize that while they're devoutly committed to religious activities, structures, and institutions, they don't have a living relationship with God.

Many today believe they are right with God simply because they are connected to a religious institution or perform religious acts such as tithing, fasting, being baptized, or eating the Lord's Supper. These people aren't terrorists, child molesters, or thieves. They're decent and devout people who spend their time, talents, energy, and money doing things for God. Yet they can wrongly conclude that because of their religious deeds, they have a relationship with God. The apostle Paul warned Timothy about people like this, people who have "a form of godliness but [deny] its power" (2 Timothy 3:5, NIV).

I pastor a church where several hundred people gather weekly for worship. Many come week in and week out because they know God and long to experience his presence in public worship. But I fear that some assume they know God merely because they show up regularly, enjoy the music and the message, and put some money in the offering plate.

It's possible to be in church without being "in Christ," as the New Testament describes that relationship. It's possible to be connected to religious things and institutions while remaining disconnected from God. After all, why would walking into a church make you a Christian any more than walking into a garage makes you a car?

Please understand, I'm not saying that religious activities such as church attendance and charitable giving are unimportant or unnecessary. The Bible strongly encourages children of God to invest themselves in the local church: "Let us not give up meeting together, as some are in the habit of doing, but let us encourage one another—and all the more as you see the Day approaching" (Hebrews 10:25, NIV). A real relationship with God will show itself in a real relationship with his people (more on this in chapter 9). But as important as church attendance and other religious activities are, they don't necessarily mean that someone has a relationship with God.

DECEPTION 4: "I'M SPIRITUAL. ISN'T THAT ENOUGH?"

From Oprah to Madonna, Tom Cruise to Deepak Chopra, our country is full of people who seem to be serious about exploring the varieties of spiritual experience.

What might be driving our generation's evident appetite for spirituality apart from religion?[3] One explanation points to what has been lost since Enlightenment man traded in the sacred and transcendent for the natural and physical.

People today live in a "world without windows," explains sociologist Peter Berger.[4] By contrast, he says, in centuries past humanity lived with windows to other worlds. They recognized there was Someone bigger, Someone to appeal to beyond themselves, a larger purpose to life beyond this world. But the modern world, with all its technological advances and scientific sophistication, has turned away from the supernatural and closed the blinds on the unseen world.

In our new world without windows, God, spirituality, and mystery have become less and less imaginable. Everything has become a matter of human classification, calculation, and control. And since there is no reality beyond what we can see, everything is produced, managed, and solved this side of the ceiling.

It seems, though, that the human spirit will have none of it. In a world robbed of mystery, people yearn for transcendence. They sense there must be more to life than the bottom line, and they begin to understand that all our modern technologies and capabilities cannot make us better, more satisfied people or answer our deepest questions.

This may explain why supernatural dramas such as *X-Files, Joan of Arcadia, Medium, Ghost Whisperer, Supernatural,* and *Heroes* seem to pop up every new television season. And why people are increasingly fascinated with Eastern mysticism, angels, aliens, psychics, the afterlife, and metaphysical healing—even why the drug ecstasy is so popular among youth. Our generation is crying out for something different, something higher, something out of this world.

This is both good and bad. As C. S. Lewis said in *Mere Christianity,* "If I find in myself a desire which no experience in this world can satisfy, the most probable explanation is that I was made for another world." People growing more conscious of the eternity that God has set in every human heart (Ecclesiastes 3:11) is a good thing, and it's something we should all celebrate. On the other hand, "people who have been starved of water for a long time will drink anything, even if it is polluted."[5] There are endless varieties of spiritual options available to people today, and spiritual seekers seem willing to try them to satisfy their spiritual thirst.

The Bible warns against any kind of spirituality apart from

true relationship with God. Time and again God condemned pagan idolatry, mysticism, and false worship. Paul wrote, "They exchanged the truth about God for a lie and worshiped and served the creature rather than the Creator" (Romans 1:25). And when Paul visited Athens and addressed the people in the Areopagus, he acknowledged how spiritual they were, yet he showed them that while they were deeply spiritual, they didn't have a relationship with the living God (Acts 17:22–31).

It's encouraging that so many people are rediscovering their spiritual thirst and are open to spiritual answers to their deepest questions and longings. But just as salt water can't quench our physical thirst, so false and incomplete spirituality can never satisfy our spiritual thirst. Only true relationship with God through faith in Jesus Christ can satisfy that thirst. True spirituality is the inner experience of an ever-deepening relationship with God the Father, through God the Son, in God the Spirit. Anything less than entering into an eternal relationship with God through Jesus Christ is a false spirituality that cannot save or satisfy.

When we settle for anything less than true spirituality, we are, Lewis said, "like an ignorant child who wants to go on making mud pies in a slum because he cannot imagine what is meant by the offer of a holiday at the sea. We are far too easily pleased."

Far better to allow our spiritual longings to bring us to Christ. Hebrews 12:2 tells us to "[look] to Jesus, the founder and perfecter of our faith, who for the joy that was set before him endured the cross, despising the shame, and is seated at the right hand of the throne of God." In Jesus we begin to understand that this world is not all there is, and he empowers us to live in this world with the next world in view. When we place our faith in Christ and what he accomplished on that "old rugged cross," he not only satisfies our thirst for God, but he also promises to usher us from this world to the next one safely and soundly—the true home where God's children will live with him forever.

5

Working *For,*
Working *Out*

What is the relationship between saving faith
and good works?

Faith alone saves,
but the faith that saves is never alone.

—Martin Luther

Cliff, the father of a close friend of mine, was one of the
kindest, gentlest men I have ever known. He embodied
Jesus's words that "it is more blessed to give than to receive" (Acts
20:35). Cliff was the kind of man whose greatest joy was to make
sure everyone around him was happy, comfortable, and well
taken care of. He regularly ran errands for friends and family, ate
lunch with his aging mother, and chauffeured his kids around

town. He loved planning birthday parties and surprising his family with gifts. And later in his life, one of his greatest joys was baby-sitting and playing with his grandkids.

Cliff's parents instilled in him strong moral and spiritual values that shaped his whole life. If a relationship with God depended on goodness and moral virtue, Cliff was a shoo-in. Sadly, that's what he believed. That is, Cliff believed that if he could live a good enough life and serve his friends and family well, he would make God happy. By making God happy, he would avoid hell and spend eternity in heaven.

But as Cliff grew older, an unsettling realization set in. He saw that he wasn't good enough for a perfect God and that no matter how hard he tried, he never would be. The thought plagued him. He was a devoted husband, father, son, brother, friend, and worker, but deep inside he knew he was flawed.

One night Cliff, his son and daughter-in-law, and I watched a Billy Graham special on television. At the end, when my granddad invited anyone who wanted to begin a relationship with God to come forward, Cliff told me how much he admired those who responded. "I wish I could make that commitment," he said, "but I'm not good enough or strong enough." Nothing his son or I said in that moment persuaded Cliff that salvation was a free gift from God. He was sure he needed to earn a relationship with God—and tragically, he was also sure he couldn't.

A few years later Cliff suffered a heart attack, slipped into a coma, and died the following day. My friend said it was one of the saddest days of his life, not only because he lost a loving father, but also because Cliff never seemed to grasp that no one can ever *achieve* a relationship with God. We can only *receive* a relationship with him through faith in what Jesus Christ has already done.

Theologically speaking, Cliff never understood the relationship between faith and works. He believed he would spend eternity with God if at the end of his life the good things he did outweighed the bad things. His relationship with God depended, he thought, on his living an upright, honest, and worthy life. Then his good works would lead to saving faith for him.

The Bible, however, teaches something different: that a person's saving faith leads to good works. Thankfully, because "salvation belongs to the LORD" (Jonah 2:9), my friend and his wife can hold on to the hope that somehow at the end God got through to Cliff. They understand that even when people are on their deathbed, God has the power to grant repentance and relieve sinners of their burden.

In the last chapter, I told you about Howard, who believes that his religious devotion to the church is all God expects from him. He believes that if God exists, God will welcome him into heaven one day because of his religious devotion. Cliff had a similar problem: he believed that his good works—if he could just pile up enough of them—could earn him a favorable relationship with God for eternity. Cliff didn't depend on his religious devotion so much as on his good deeds and moral virtue, serving his friends and family, treating everyone fairly, never cheating or intentionally hurting anyone, and so on.

In this chapter I invite you to wrestle with what we could call Cliff's Conundrum: *If I can please God by living a good enough life, how good do I have to be? And if all my good works can't bring me into relationship with God, then what does? And if I can't ever be good enough, then what's the point of even trying?*

In other words, I want to explore why it's impossible for you to live a good enough life to please God. Then we'll explore an apparent paradox: for us as children of God, our good works really do matter.

DECEPTION 5: "I'M A GOOD PERSON. ISN'T THAT ENOUGH?"

In Romans the apostle Paul said something that seems at first glance to be downright inaccurate. He said that no one does good. Referring to a number of Old Testament verses, he wrote:

> "None is righteous, no, not one;
>> no one understands;
>> no one seeks for God.

All have turned aside; together they have become worthless;
    no one does good,
        not even one."
"Their throat is an open grave;
    they use their tongues to deceive."
"The venom of asps is under their lips."
        "Their mouth is full of curses and bitterness."
"Their feet are swift to shed blood;
    in their paths are ruin and misery,
and the way of peace they have not known."
        "There is no fear of God before their eyes."
            (Romans 3:10–18)

No one does good? *No one?* Surely there are kind mothers, faithful fathers, obedient children, and honest businesspeople out there.

Yes, there are. And Paul wouldn't argue with that. But when the Bible speaks about a "good work," it means specifically a good work that is motivated by love for God. It is an act of moral virtue done with a purpose: to glorify God. That's why Jesus condemned the Pharisees' so-called good works:

Woe to you, scribes and Pharisees, hypocrites! For you
clean the outside of the cup and the plate, but inside they

are full of greed and self-indulgence. You blind Pharisee!
First clean the inside of the cup and the plate, that the
outside also may be clean.

Woe to you, scribes and Pharisees, hypocrites! For
you are like whitewashed tombs, which outwardly appear
beautiful, but within are full of dead people's bones and
all uncleanness. So you also outwardly appear righteous to
others, but within you are full of hypocrisy and lawlessness. (Matthew 23:25–28)

Jesus admitted that the Pharisees' works looked beautiful on
the outside, but inside, those Pharisees were spiritually dead.
They weren't motivated to do good out of love for God or a desire
to glorify him.

In the same way, you and I see admirable people who do
admirable things for families, friends, communities, and the poor.
But unless those admirable deeds are motivated by love for God
and have as their goal the glory of God, they cannot be consid-
ered good in an ultimate sense. Only someone who has a heart
for God can do good in this sense. The problem is, as we've seen,
we can't gain a heart for God on our own. Only an act of God
can remove our "heart of stone" and give us a "heart of flesh"
(Ezekiel 11:19). This is why the prophet Isaiah said that, apart
from God, "all our righteous deeds are like a polluted garment"

(Isaiah 64:6). Our only hope is to place our faith in what Jesus Christ has already done.

This beautiful, liberating truth raises two questions. First, what has Christ done? And second, what is faith?

Let's start with the first.

What Has Christ Done?

The foundational notion behind every world religion except Christianity is humanity's ascent to God. They are all, to one degree or another, bottom-up religions; they require believers to work their way up into a relationship with the divine, however that idea is understood. Believers can attain salvation only by trying harder. Everything depends on individual effort.

In contrast, the foundation of Christianity is God's gracious descent to humanity. "The Word *became* flesh and dwelt among us" (John 1:14, emphasis added). Christianity is not a bottom-up religion but a top-down relationship: "God so loved the world, that he *gave* his only Son, that whoever believes in him should not perish but have eternal life" (John 3:16, emphasis added). God descended to us in the person of Jesus Christ because we could not ascend to him. In Jesus, God physically came into our world to rescue us from the penalty, power, and eventually the presence of sin.

As we saw in chapter 2, because of sin, we're born without a saving relationship to our Creator. Ephesians 2:1 tells us that we are born dead in our trespasses and sins. Due to sin, none of us can choose God or love him on our own. We are morally, spiritually, and relationally dead to God.

Theologians use two words to describe this deformity of our natures: *total depravity.* I doubt Cliff would have used words like that to describe his spiritual struggles, but he deeply felt their reality nonetheless.

Total depravity does not mean utter depravity. Utter depravity means that someone is as bad as he or she could possibly be. Thankfully, God graciously prevents even the worst of us from becoming utterly depraved—we could all be worse. Total depravity, on the other hand, means that sin has corrupted us in the totality of our being.

In other words, sin affects every part of us. Sin corrupts all our thoughts, all our feelings, and all our behavior. Nothing we think, feel, or do is as good as it should be. So, contrary to what positive thinkers and some psychologists would have us think, humans are not fine just the way we are. Paul wrote that apart from Christ we're hostile toward God; we don't want to choose him (Romans 8:7–8). (Do you see why it's impossible for people to work themselves into a relationship with God?)

This brings us back to what Jesus Christ has done to make a relationship with God possible. Paul wrote, "A person is not justified by works of the law but through faith in Jesus Christ, so we also have believed in Christ Jesus, in order to be justified by faith in Christ and not by works of the law, because by works of the law no one will be justified" (Galatians 2:16).

Justification is a legal term that, in Paul's time, was commonly heard in courtrooms. To justify someone was to declare that person innocent, acquitted of all charges.

What does this legal term have to do with working our way toward God? You and I stand guilty in God's courtroom. And God is the only one with the power to declare us guilt free.

But God's pardon comes at a great cost. A just God could not ignore or overlook sin and remain just. Sin is a serious offense that requires a serious penalty. In order for someone to enter into a relationship with God, God requires payment for that person's sin, and the payment is death (Romans 6:23). But since the penalty for offending an infinite, holy God requires an infinite, perfect price, then God—and only God—can pay it. And that's where the cross of Jesus Christ comes in: the only reason God can adopt you and me into his family forever is because of Christ's sacrifice. None of our so-called goodness has anything to do with it.

Perhaps now you see why down through the centuries the cross of Jesus Christ has stood at the center of what Christians believe about God and the relationship he offers to sinners like you and me. The cross reminds us of our great sickness while at the same time reminding us of God's great salvation. Christ did for sinners what sinners could never do for themselves. This is the gospel, the good news.

In his remarkable book *Jesus Ascended,* Gerrit Scott Dawson gives an illustration that might help you understand what Christ accomplished.

> A child is conceived through the loving communion of husband and wife. The child grows inside the sheltering womb of the mother. But the wee one cannot live there for ever. He is made for another world, a world of daylight and air, starlight and sky. So in the hours of her labour, the mother offers a new and living way. The way to life as a human being in the world passes through the curtain of her flesh.... The curtain must be torn that the child might live and reach the daylight world. She is the new and living way. By her pain, the child is born.[1]

That's exactly how the Bible speaks of Christ's work on the cross. In the same way we were brought into this world through the pain and suffering of our mothers, Christ delivers sinners into fellowship with God through his own pain and suffering. The way to everlasting life passes through the curtain of Christ's flesh.

So God's gift to the world was to send Jesus into the world to reconcile sinners to himself and invite them into an eternal relationship with him. The only way to obtain that eternal gift is to believe. The Bible says, "Without faith it is impossible to please

God" (Hebrews 11:6, NIV). That's the part Cliff never quite grasped.

But now we must explore what the Bible means when it refers to faith.

What Is Faith?

The Bible defines faith as "the assurance of things hoped for, the conviction of things not seen" (Hebrews 11:1). Faith is believing with the eyes of your heart what you cannot see with the eyes of your head. In regard to a relationship with God, "faith is transferring your trust from your own efforts to the efforts of Christ," says Tim Keller, pastor of Redeemer Presbyterian Church in New York City.

This faith, however, is no blind leap in the dark. Far from it. The Bible teaches that faith is an exercise of reasonable trust in a God who is really there and has proved himself to be completely trustworthy. In fact, it would be utterly unreasonable and irrational *not* to trust in someone who has proved himself to be infinitely dependable. The whole Bible bears witness to the reality that God has been, is now, and will always be truthful and worthy of our trust. We may not always understand what God is doing or why he is doing it, but we have no good reason to doubt him.

But what does all this talk of faith (or lack of it) have to do with Christ's work on the cross? Just this: in order for someone to enter into a relationship with him, God requires faith in what Christ did on the cross for sinners. Relationship with God depends on our whole-souled response to what Christ has done. A true step of faith involves believing in Christ's work with our minds, embracing it with our affections, and trusting it with our wills. Christ's sacrifice on the cross all by itself does not bring us into a relationship with God. (Think about how many people dismiss who Christ is and ignore his work on the cross!) You and I must *act*. We must choose to exercise faith—reasonable trust—in what Christ accomplished on the cross in order for us to receive and experience a relationship with God, remembering, of course, that faith *itself* is a gift from God (Ephesians 2:8–9) and that the only way we can love him is if he first loves us (1 John 4:19). But, as John Calvin reminds us, "As long as Christ remains outside of us, and we are separated from him, all that he has suffered and done for the salvation of the human race remains useless and of no value for us."

We've seen that all our good works are worthless in terms of winning us an eternal relationship with God. But does that mean the good things we do count for nothing in this world? If faith is all it takes to spend eternity with God, why bother trying to be good?

These questions lead us to the last common misunderstanding about how we can truly know God.

DECEPTION 6: "BUT I HAVE FAITH. ISN'T THAT ENOUGH?"

It's absolutely true: we can enter into an eternal relationship with God only through faith in Jesus Christ and what he accomplished on the cross. God rescues us; we don't rescue ourselves. We don't deserve salvation, and we can't earn it. But that doesn't mean that once we enter into a relationship with God, he doesn't require any effort from us.

I once heard someone say there are always two ways to fall off a tightrope. In other words, there are always two extremes to avoid. In relation to faith and justification, we've already examined the first extreme to avoid: that we must *work for* our relationship to God. Now let's look at the second extreme to avoid: that we don't need to *work out* our relationship to God.

The Bible identifies two types of faith in God. The first is living faith.

> By this we know that we have come to know him, if we keep his commandments. (1 John 2:3)

> My beloved, as you have always obeyed, so now, not only as in my presence but much more in my absence, work out your own salvation with fear and trembling, for it is

God who works in you, both to will and to work for his good pleasure. (Philippians 2:12–13)

And then there is dead faith.

Whoever says "I know him" but does not keep his commandments is a liar, and the truth is not in him. (1 John 2:4)

What good is it, my brothers, if someone says he has faith but does not have works? Can that faith save him? If a brother or sister is poorly clothed and lacking in daily food, and one of you says to them, "Go in peace, be warmed and filled," without giving them the things needed for the body, what good is that? So also faith by itself, if it does not have works, is dead. (James 2:14–17)

Dead faith is faith in God that doesn't lead to a changed life. People with dead faith profess to believe in Christ, but their lives haven't changed. These are people who talk the talk but don't walk the walk. Paul said these are people who "profess to know God, but they deny him by their works" (Titus 1:16).

Remember Jason in chapter 3? Jason was a young man I met a few years ago who was living with a woman who attended my church. He professed to have faith in Jesus because several years earlier he had prayed the sinner's prayer at a Christian youth conference. But he had shown no interest in living a godly life. His spiritual condition hadn't changed one bit, and he demonstrated no interest in its changing. Based on almost every evidence, we could conclude that Jason's faith is dead.

Living faith, on the other hand, is faith in God that leads to genuine life changes. People with living faith express it in and through their thoughts, affections, and actions. It completely changes how someone lives and what he loves. To be sure, living faith is not perfect faith that shows itself in perfect living, but it is active faith. As Ralph Erskine said, "Faith without trouble or fighting is a suspicious faith; for true faith is a fighting, wrestling faith." Living faith is faith that works.

My seminary years were some of the best years of my life. But there were times when my friends and I started to believe that what we were learning was more important than whether we were actually living it. Knowing the right stuff trumped doing the right thing. We started to think that Christians who refused to drink, smoke, curse, and watch movies were weak and silly. We, on the other hand, represented a more muscular Christianity—a Christianity that put serious thinking about God above serious living for God. We forgot that the two things can't be separated. The Bible never builds a wall between what we believe and how we live. What we believe has everything to do with how we live, and how we live has everything to do with what we believe.

Today, as a pastor, I talk to people all the time who fall into a similar trap. They understand perfectly that no one can earn a relationship with God through good works. They have no doubt we are saved by grace, "and this not from yourselves, it is the gift of God—not by works, so that no one can boast" (Ephesians 2:8–9, NIV). But convinced of this truth, they go to the extreme and become careless about good works altogether. In effect, they're singing the anthem

> Free from the law,
> O blessed condition;
> I can sin as I please
> and still have remission.

Throughout history a misunderstanding about the connection between faith and works has caused tremendous confusion and led to dangerous extremes. For example, in the 1950s, many churches in America practiced a strict, legalistic, behavior-focused version of Christianity that reduced knowing God to little more than adhering to a strict set of rules and regulations. As a result, several Christian movements rose up in the 1960s, particularly among youth, that emphasized a faith that was more focused on God's love and grace, his forgiveness and mercy. Sadly, some went too far and took God's grace as a license to sin. And as a result, some of the leaders of these movements ended up out of the ministry altogether because of extramarital affairs, financial indiscretion, and other moral failures. Events like these can warn us of the serious consequences we should expect when we think that because of God's grace and mercy, we don't need to live up to his holy standards.

The Bible is clear that salvation comes through faith alone. But at the same time, it never says you and I can do whatever we want to do and live however we want to live and still possess true assurance that we have a relationship with God. Faith is essential to the Christian life—and so is right behavior.

FAITH AND WORKS ARE BOTH ESSENTIAL

Some followers of Christ are confused about the role of good works in the Christian life because of the apparent contradiction between what the apostles James and Paul said about it.

Paul, especially in Galatians, seems to have taken a negative view of works. For example, going back to Galatians 2:16, Paul said, "We know that a person is not justified by works of the law but through faith in Jesus Christ, so we also have believed in Christ Jesus, in order to be justified by faith in Christ and not by works of the law, because by works of the law no one will be justified." He also said, "It is by grace you have been saved, through faith— and this not from yourselves, it is the gift of God—not by works, so that no one can boast" (Ephesians 2:8–9, NIV).

James, on the other hand, seems to have thought that works

are not only important but essential in our relationship to God. In his letter he said, "Faith by itself, if it does not have works, is dead," and "A person is justified by works and not by faith alone," and "Faith apart from works is dead" (James 2:17, 24, 26).

So are works necessary or not? Who's right—Paul or James?

A good place to start resolving these apparent contradictions is to understand that James and Paul were writing to different audiences. Paul was writing to a group of Christians who had started to believe (because of some false teachers in their midst) that they had to meet certain conditions in order to earn a relationship with God. Paul wrote his letter to the Galatians to correct them, teaching them that salvation depends entirely on God. No one can earn a relationship with God. James, on the other hand, wrote to a group of Christians facing brutal persecution. James wrote his letter to encourage them not to give up but to press on. Throughout his letter James made the point that when things get tough, what we do demonstrates who we are better than what we say. As Alan Redpath said, "The flavor of a teabag only comes out when put in hot water."

What Paul and James had to say about faith and works are not contradictory at all. In fact, they are complementary. Paul talked about the role of works in becoming a child of God; James talked about the role of works in being a child of God. Put another way, Paul said it's impossible to "work for" a relationship to God; James said it's necessary to "work out" a relationship to God. James and Paul agreed that works have nothing to do with spiritual birth. Works do, however, have everything to do with spiritual growth. James and Paul agreed that saving faith and good works are inseparable: saving faith inevitably produces good works.

Christians throughout history have explained the relationship between saving faith and good works in this way: faith alone saves, but the faith that saves is never alone. If you are truly a child of God, your relationship with him will express itself in a radically transformed life. Real faith always leads to real fruit. Paul urged in Philippians 2, "Work out your own salvation with fear and trembling" (verse 12). But he added that "it is God who works in you, both to will and to work for his good pleasure" (verse 13). When God adopts you into his family, he plants within you new thoughts and desires, and then he expects you to live out the changes he makes within you. This is one of the most important ways to tell whether you are truly a child of God (more about this in chapter 8). A true relationship with God changes everything about you. And, to put it another way, a relationship with God that does not change everything about you is not a relationship with God.

Finding certainty in life's most important relationship involves a whole-souled determination to work out one's salvation with fear and trembling. As we do this, God will satisfy the inner certainty we all crave.

Over the past three chapters we've covered a lot of ground, looking at six ways people deceive themselves into thinking they know God and will spend eternity with him when they really won't.

1. It's not enough just to pray the sinner's prayer or walk forward during an evangelistic invitation.

2. It's not enough to simply remember a time in your past when you made a decision for Jesus Christ.

3. It's not enough just to attend church, tithe, teach Sunday school, preach sermons, or commit yourself to religious activities.

4. It's not enough to dive into spiritual experiences apart from relationship with the living God.

5. It's not enough to live a good life or be a good person.

6. It's not enough to profess that you have faith in Christ if your life never shows any evidence of new life.

Now that we've seen what a Christian is not, let's turn our attention to three ways you can know that you know God.

In the next three chapters we'll discover that if our relationship to God is real, it will show itself in the way we think, the way we feel, and the way we live. If you truly know God, you will believe God's promises with your head (chapter 6), desire God's purposes in your heart (chapter 7), and obey God's precepts with your hands (chapter 8). These are the three "vital signs" that let us know that our relationship to God is genuine.

6

The Weight of His Word

How does believing the promises of God
assure me of my salvation?

*It is the word of God alone which can first
and effectually cheer the heart of the sinner.
There is no true or solid peace to be enjoyed
in the world except in the way of resting
upon the promises of God.*
—JOHN CALVIN

You've heard the business adage that says a promise is only
as good as the business behind it. The same is true in our
personal lives. A promise is only as good as the character of the
person who makes the promise.

And if it's true of businesses and people, shouldn't we be able to hold God to the same principle?

Do you believe that God will keep his promises to you? And do you know him well enough to trust the person behind the promise? We'll explore questions like these in the chapter ahead.

Consider marriage as a high-stakes relationship in which promises and persons meet. When you enter into a marriage with someone and recite your sacred vows, you trust that your partner is going to keep his or her vow. You trust that your mate will keep his or her promise. Why? Because you have come to know your spouse. You know this person's character, motives, record, and heart.

Still, this placing of trust—this letting down of suspicions and safeguards—is risky. It's part of the human experience to be hurt by someone or something we've put our trust in. We've all been wounded by people who promised to change, promised to deliver, promised to watch our back, promised to be there when we needed them. And they broke their promises. Husbands, wives, boyfriends, girlfriends, employers, employees, friends, pastors, and even our own children—they dashed our hopes, abused our trust, violated our sense of loyalty. We end up asking, "Is there anyone I can trust?"

I recently witnessed the heartbreak of another broken promise. One of my best friends, Dave, called the other day to tell me that, after forty-one years of marriage, his parents were divorcing. He was devastated, and I was shocked. They were like family to me. The strange thing is, there was no physical abuse, no marital infidelity. In fact, to many people, Dave's parents modeled authentic Christianity. There's nothing hypocritical about them. They're real, and they both love God passionately.

Dave said it almost destroyed him to tell his nine-year-old son, Josh. He took the boy out to lunch and said, "Josh, I have some really sad news. Grandma and Grandpa are getting divorced."

Shocked and confused, Josh launched into a bunch of questions. "Aren't Grandma and Grandpa Christians?"

"Yes," Dave said.

"Isn't divorce bad?"

"Yes," he replied.

"Didn't they promise never to get a divorce?"

"Yes," he replied once more.

Then Josh laid his head on the table and cried—and Dave cried with him. Dave and his son both feel the painful disappointment of watching two people they love unable to keep their promises to each other. I suspect it's going to take them a long time to recover from that disappointment. For Dave, his son, and the rest of his family, life will never be the same.

If a promise is only as good as the character of the one who makes that promise, then we'd have to conclude that, because of sin, no one's character is good enough to guarantee security. We've all broken promises, and we've all suffered the consequences.

But what about God? Is God's character good enough that we can trust his promises? The Bible takes this question seriously, and it reveals to us a God who invites—and merits—our absolute confidence. God never breaks promises; he never lies (Titus 1:2). When he makes promises, we can trust them without question, for they are absolutely right and true (Numbers 23:19). With him, our hearts and our hopes are forever safe. J. I. Packer wrote, "The words of human beings are unstable things, but not so the words of God."

If we're going to enter into a love relationship with God and experience the certainty he promises, the place to start is to get to know this God—his character and his heart. From there, if we're persuaded by what we learn, we can more naturally move to a settled trust that he'll keep his promises.

But as you'll see, that is still just a beginning. To *experience* the certainty that we have a relationship with God, we must begin to believe God's promises.

God has made stunning relational promises to sinners like you and me, and knowing that you know God requires you to believe that these promises are for you. And because of God's character, we can be certain God will never fail nor falter in what he's promised to do.

Over the past three chapters, I showed you six reasons that might lead you to question whether you know God. But in this chapter and the next two, I want to show you three ways you can *know* that you know him. I'm going to introduce you to God and his character, and then we'll look more closely at the promises of God you can build your life on.

THE CHARACTER OF THE PROMISER

Over the past several years, social researchers have consistently found that 85 to 90 percent of Americans believe in God. But who is this divine being they say they believe in? A recent study out of Baylor University found that Americans actually believe in one of four different gods. "Americans may agree that God exists. They do not agree on what God is like [or] what God wants for the world."[1] The study gave each God a different name based on the dominant characteristic respondents used to describe their deity:

- *The Authoritarian God*—a God who is both judgmental and directly engaged with the world.
- *The Benevolent God*—a God who is not judgmental but still intervenes actively in our lives.
- *The Distant God*—a God who doesn't interact much, if at all, in our lives.
- *The Critical God*—a God who doesn't intervene in our lives but who is nonetheless displeased with what we're doing in the world.

These results suggest several important insights for our discussion here. For one thing, we should realize that when we talk about

God, what we communicate may be received in an entirely different way from what we intended. For another, based on the range and generally negative slant of the descriptions of God, we shouldn't be surprised when people show reluctance to trust him with their lives. And finally, a lot of American Christians clearly do not really know the God they profess to believe in!

With the help of the Bible, let's examine the real character of God to see whether we can take him at his word. We'll look briefly at three attributes, or characteristics, of God that will give us the confidence we need to believe his promises.

God Is Independent

There's a fundamental difference between God and us: he is the Creator, and we are his creatures. This means that God is absolutely independent. He needs nothing outside himself in order to exist. He is self-sufficient and self-contained.

On the other hand, you and I are completely dependent on God. We're not self-sufficient or self-contained. We're fragile. Tragedies such as tsunamis, hurricanes, terrorist attacks, AIDS, and cancer constantly remind us that we're far more breakable and vulnerable than we like to admit. We need air, food, and water. We couldn't last five minutes without God's gracious provision for our most basic needs.

We depend on God not only for physical things but also for knowledge, for understanding, and for definitions of what's right and wrong, what's true and false. Psalm 36:9 says, "In your light we see light" (NIV). Commenting on this psalm, Richard Pratt says:

> God knows all and it is upon His knowledge that we
> must depend if we ourselves are to know [anything]. Any
> true understanding which men have is derived either
> intentionally or unintentionally from God...for it is God
> who teaches knowledge (Psalm 94:10). Men do actually
> think, yet true knowledge is dependent on and derived
> from God's knowledge as it has been revealed to man.[2]

In other words, you and I cannot attain true knowledge or true understanding of anything unless God reveals it to us. R. C. Sproul summed it up well: "The grand difference between a human being and a Supreme Being is precisely this: Apart from God I cannot exist; apart from me God does exist. God does not need me in order for him to be. I do need God in order for me to be."[3]

So how does God's independence affect his trustworthiness in our lives? God's independence assures us he will keep his promises because it means nothing can ever get in God's way, and nothing can stop him, divert him, or thwart him.

When you and I make a promise, all kinds of things can keep us from fulfilling our promise. People can interrupt us, traffic can stop us, weather can ruin our plans. If I promise to take my two boys to a Miami Heat basketball game on Friday, but I come down with the flu on Thursday, I won't be able to keep my promise. We're all dependent on our circumstances to keep our promises. But because God is independent, nothing outside him can ever keep him from fulfilling his promises to us.

God Is Immutable

God never changes (Malachi 3:6). There is no need for God to change either, because he is perfect. He needs no improvements. Nothing can be added to or taken away from his faultless being. He can't learn anything more or grow wiser, because he already knows everything that can be known. God is the same "yesterday and today and forever" (Hebrews 13:8). And because God never changes, his purposes never change, his ways never change, and his promises never change.

To be sure, God interacts with and responds to his creation. He listens to our prayers; he sees our actions; he knows our hearts; he responds with compassion and wisdom. But in none of these actions does God alter his eternal purposes—or need to. What God works out in time and space is what he purposed and planned to do from all eternity (Psalm 33:11). Even when the Bible speaks of God changing his mind, it doesn't mean that he changes his ultimate purpose. It simply means that he chooses to deal with someone in a new way. But this new way doesn't imply a change from what he planned to do all along. It's new from our perspective, not from God's.

Unlike God, however, everything he created changes all the time. Creation is not immutable. As the Greek philosopher Heraclitus famously said, "You cannot step into the same river twice." In other words, everything is in a state of flux; nothing stays the same. The ocean tides change; weather patterns change; the colors of leaves change. And people change constantly in every way: we get older, weaker, stronger, fatter, skinnier. Our thinking, feelings, and actions change daily because we have flaws, shortcomings, weaknesses that we need to change. All of us need improvement.

But God does not. He has no weaknesses; he needs no improvements. He is immutable. This means that, unlike you and me, God never changes his mind about his ultimate purposes. God made a promise to sinners that if we unconditionally surrender our lives to him, we can enter into a love relationship with him forever. And God will keep his promise.

God Is Infinite

When I was a kid, one of my friends asked me, "What's the biggest number?"

I said something like, "A trillion, dummy."

He quickly corrected me by telling me the largest number was "infinity."

I was confused. *Infinity* didn't sound like any number I had ever heard before.

I was right. Infinity isn't a number. The word *infinite* means "having no limits" or "extending without boundaries."

It's hard for people like you and me to grasp infinity. We're creatures bound by time. We were born, and we will die, and everything we do in between—meals, vacations, pregnancies, thoughts, sleep, play—takes place within the scope of time. All of it has a beginning and an end.

But God is infinite. He has no beginning, and he has no end. As the psalmist wrote,

> Before the mountains were brought forth,
> > or ever you had formed the earth and the world,
> > from everlasting to everlasting you are God....
> For a thousand years in your sight
> > are but as yesterday when it is past,
> > or as a watch in the night. (Psalm 90:2, 4)

God, however, is not only infinite in regard to time, but he's also infinite in regard to space. God is omnipresent—he's everywhere, in all places at all times. David described it like this:

> Where shall I go from your Spirit?
> > Or where shall I flee from your presence?

If I ascend to heaven, you are there!
 If I make my bed in Sheol, you are there!
If I take the wings of the morning
 and dwell in the uttermost parts of the sea,
even there your hand shall lead me,
 and your right hand shall hold me. (Psalm 139:7–10)

Now think about how important God's infinity is to you in terms of God's keeping his promises. Time and space, for example, can be big problems when you and I try to keep our promises. If I tell my wife that I'll pick up our son Nathan from football practice at five o'clock, and I get stuck in traffic, then I am physically incapable of keeping my word. I can't be in more than one place at one time, so there will be occasions when I'll make a promise I can't keep. Time, however, is never a problem for God, and he can always be, not only in two places at the same time, but everywhere at the same time.

This is important because it means that Gods knows everything about the past, present, and future simultaneously. You and I cannot know everything. Our knowledge of the past and present is partial and vague. Our knowledge of the future is fractional and general. Yes, we know we're going to die, but none of us knows when. We know Christ will return one day, but we don't know when.

But God does.

So What?

Those big words—*independent, immutable,* and *infinite*—are difficult to wrap our minds around. But what these characteristics of God add up to is this: God is morally and physically incapable of breaking his promises. He's morally incapable of breaking his promises because he's perfect. God cannot sin. For God to break his promise, he would have to cease being God. And God cannot stop being God. He's physically incapable of breaking his promises because he can do all things, know all things, and be all places without any physical restrictions or boundaries. So while human beings often break their promises, God's promises will never fail, because of who he is.

We can trust God's promises because they are founded on and grounded in his own perfectly independent, immutable, and infinite being. But that's not the only reason we can trust God's promises.

TRUSTING GOD BECAUSE HE LOVES US

As we have seen, God is big. He is independent, immutable, and infinite. These are the attributes of God that theologians and philosophers collectively call his *transcendent attributes*—a fancy phrase that describes how radically different God is from us. When you encounter God's transcendence, you fall on your knees in awe before God's overwhelming majesty, his exalted greatness, his eternal immensity.

You can trust a God that big to keep his promises. But in the presence of God's greatness and power, it's easy to forget that he is not some generically grand, impersonal cosmic ideal. We don't trust God to keep his promises merely because he's so big; we also trust God because he's so personal. We trust God because he is love.

God is deeply personal—so personal that he created us to know him and to be known by him. In fact, at the risk of sounding flippant, God is the consummate "people person." Theologians would put this wonderful truth this way: God is not only transcendent, but he is also immanent. That is, as immanent, he is near to everything and everyone he has made. He is intimately concerned with and involved in the affairs of all his children for all time.

Those who know God fall into the open arms of a heavenly Father who is merciful and compassionate. He is tender, slow to anger, and abounding in love—a love so unrelenting, deep, and intense that he'll track us down even when we are running from him. He knows every detail of our lives, and he's more aware of our darkest sins than we are. Yet he loves us just the same with a love so full that we find we never need anything more.

"God is our refuge and strength, a very present help in trouble"

(Psalm 46:1), the one who both cares for and comes to the aid of those who cling to him. In fact, there is no greater expression of God's love than the amazing grace and kindness he shows by saving sinners like you and me from judgment and death. This was a love that cost Jesus Christ his life on the cross at Calvary (Romans 3:22–24; 5:5–8; 8:32–39; Ephesians 2:1–10; 3:14–19; 5:25–27). As Jesus himself said, "Greater love has no one than this, that someone lays down his life for his friends. You are my friends" (John 15:13–14).

That's a God we can trust to keep his word.

Unfortunately many people feel as if God has broken promises to them. Experiencing that kind of disappointment with God can crush our spirits. But what if the problem is that we expect God to keep promises he never made?

Claire, a member of our church, recently came to visit me in total disarray. She told me about the past ten painful, dreadful years of her life. Then she turned to me and asked, "Can't I expect this pain to go away? Why does God continue to allow me to suffer? Doesn't he promise good things to those who know him?"

I know that pain. I really do. And I've asked those same questions many times in my life. But I'm finally beginning to understand that maybe I expect God to do things he never promised to do. For that matter, we all do. We expect (even when we don't express it) God to bless us with pain-free lives, low-maintenance marriages, well-behaved kids, plenty of money, and more pleasure than pain. And when God doesn't come through, we find ourselves sorely disappointed in him.

Too many people fall into the trap of believing that God is some kind of cosmic genie in a bottle. Or we expect that he owes us something whenever we do something good for him. But as Pastor Tim Keller says, "That is not Christianity at all, but a form of paganism in which you appease the cranky deity to get a favor."

I have found myself many times accusing God of breaking promises he never made. The truth is, God never promised to deliver us from affliction here and now, even if we're really good. Sometimes he chooses to intervene in our circumstances and relieve our pain. And when he does, we rejoice. But it always helps me to remember Psalm 46:1: "God is…a very present help in trouble"—not *from* trouble. Or as Henry Durbanville once said, "We have been promised a safe arrival but not a smooth voyage." Thankfully, as Claire came to accept this truth, she found tremendous comfort in it.

The fact is, God promises something bigger, better, deeper, and brighter than an easy passage through this life. Let's look further at what God promises to save us from and save us to.

The Character of the Promise

God promises to save us from wrath. I remember sharing the need to be saved with a college guy in my office. He looked at me and said, "You Christians always talk about the need to be saved. I don't understand. Saved from what?"

Paul said that Jesus "rescues us from the coming wrath" (1 Thessalonians 1:10, NIV). In other words, Jesus came to save us from God! The last person an unrepentant, Christless sinner wants to meet after he or she dies is God. As it says in Hebrews 10:31, "It is a fearful thing to fall into the hands of the living God." Everyone who dies still separated from God faces an eternity of doom and gloom.

The good news, however, is that no one needs to remain separated from God. The wonder of the gospel is that the one who promises us wrath is the same one who saves us from it. Christ came to absorb God's wrath on behalf of God's children. Therefore, God promises that when we put our trust in Christ for salvation, we are saved forever from the coming wrath. Edward T. Welch said, "The gospel is the story of God covering his naked enemies, bringing them to the wedding feast, and then marrying them rather than crushing them."

It's no wonder Christians call this message the "gospel"— good news.

God promises to save us to a new family. He not only promises that when we put our trust in Christ, we are saved forever from the coming wrath, but God also reconciles us to himself and (as I explained in chapter 2) adopts us as his own children. God brings us into a close, personal, everlasting relationship with himself—a relationship that promises both fatherly care and fatherly discipline (Matthew 6:26; Hebrews 12:5–11).

For some people, God's promise to be a Father is difficult to embrace. Maybe you're one of those people. Perhaps your earthly father let you down so badly that the very idea of gaining a new Father sounds painful. But deep inside, we all intuitively know what a *good* father does and doesn't do. Our disappointment with bad fathers proves it. We wouldn't be disappointed if we didn't carry within us the image of an ideal father.

And God is that ideal heavenly Father. He promises to never let his children down (Matthew 7:11). He promises to fully satisfy our deepest longings and expectations of what a father ought to be and do (Mathew 6:26). He promises to protect us and provide for us. He's never too busy, and he's always near. He promises to be the Father we always longed for, and nothing will ever separate us from his love or from his family (Romans 8:39).

When God adopts us, we not only gain a Father, but we also gain a family: the church. "You are no longer strangers and aliens, but you are fellow citizens with the saints and *members of the household of God*," Paul said (Ephesians 2:19, emphasis added).

The biblical word for "church" does not mean a building or institution; it means "the called-out ones." It refers to those whom God calls out of slavery and into sonship or daughtership. The church, in other words, is people—people adopted by God, people who know God as their heavenly Father. When God saves sinners, he saves them into a whole new community—the family of God. As Frank Colquhoun writes in his book *Total Christianity*, "When Christ saves a man he not only saves him from his *sin,* he saves him from his *solitude.*"

He brings us into meaningful fellowship with others who will help us along the way in our relationship with God.

God promises to save us to a new purpose. Paul wrote, "Whether you eat or drink, or whatever you do, do all to the glory of God" (1 Corinthians 10:31). When God saves us, we no longer have to settle for manufacturing our own fleeting legacies. He gives us a new reason to live: to glorify him. We live, in other words, for something huge and significant: to display God, to spread his fame, and to build his everlasting kingdom. We become part of an infinitely larger story than our own personal history, and we no longer have to work for our own puny causes but instead for God's universal cause. Paul said, "We are his workmanship, created in Christ Jesus for good works, which God prepared beforehand" (Ephesians 2:10).

In his book *Orthodoxy,* G. K. Chesterton wrote, "How much larger your life would be if your self could become smaller in it." Nothing makes you more aware of your smallness and life's potential bigness than being in a relationship with the living God. God promises a big, purposeful life to everyone who knows him.

God promises to save us to a new power. When God enters

into an everlasting relationship with us, he not only promises to pardon us for the past, but he also promises us a new power for the present. Before Jesus ascended back into heaven, he told his disciples, "You will receive power when the Holy Spirit has come upon you" (Acts 1:8).

Most of us know we're imperfect and need to change. Most of us want to live better lives. But no matter how hard we try, we can't. We don't have the power to change ourselves.

But God does. In his book *The Contemporary Christian,* John Stott said, "Is God really able to change human nature…to make cruel people kind, selfish people unselfish, immoral people self-controlled, and sour people sweet? Is he able to take people who are dead to spiritual reality, and make them alive in Christ? Yes, he really is!"[4] And when God's Holy Spirit enters us, we receive all the power we need to become the people God always intended us to be. The Bible makes it clear that, in Christ, God provides us with everything we need for godliness.

In his book *Mere Christianity,* C. S. Lewis said, "God became man to turn creatures into sons: not simply to produce better men of the old kind but to produce a new kind of man. It is not like teaching a horse to jump better and better but like turning a horse into a winged creature."[5]

New, unimaginable changes await all God's children because God promises a new, unimaginable power.

WHAT YOU LOVE MOST

The good news is that the character of God's promises rests on the character of God himself. He throws his perfectly independent, immutable, infinite weight behind these promises I've just described. And that means you can count on these promises with your life. God cannot break them. When you believe that, and when you believe these eternal promises of God, you will begin to experience the assurance and the certainty that you are truly God's child.

And that leads to the second way you can experience certainty that you know God. When God adopts sinners into his family, he gives them brand-new hearts that are full of passion and love for him. What do you love most? What are your heart's deepest desires? You can be sure that your deepest desires reveal important truths about your spiritual condition.

7

A Sense of the Presence

How do my feelings for God assure me of my salvation?

The heart is known by its delights,
and pleasures never lie.

—JOHN PIPER

When I pulled up to their modest log cabin, my heart started to race. I've been visiting my grandparents at their mountain home just outside Asheville, North Carolina, my whole life. But spending time in the home of Billy and Ruth Graham continues to be a powerful experience for me. My grandparents have been walking with God for more than seventy years, and they know him better than anyone else I know. Their simple, single-hearted devotion to their Lord saturates virtually everything they say and do. Every time I spend a few days with them, I leave with a renewed passion to know God the way they do.

I walked through the front door and immediately made my way back to their bedroom, where I knew they were waiting for me. My grandfather sat in a chair next to Tai Tai (it's what I call my grandmother), who was sitting up in bed. Neither of them gets around well anymore, so they spend most of their days together in their bedroom reading, talking, and praying. When I walked into the bedroom, their faces lit up. After giving them both a hug and kiss, I sat down next to Tai Tai. They asked me about Kim, the kids, and the church. I asked them how they were doing.

As we talked, I noticed a large three-ring binder next to my grandmother. The open page contained eight or ten words in extremely large print. I asked her what it was. She told me that because her vision is so bad now, she had asked her assistant to type up all 150 psalms in big, bold letters and put them in three-ring binders. She pointed to her shelf, where there were at least ten more binders containing the rest of the psalms. Every day she sits in bed, incapable of moving on her own, meditating on and memorizing those psalms.

That image, testifying to her passion for God, affected me profoundly. My grandmother is in her late eighties, with severe physical limitations, but she still pursues fellowship with God with every last bit of energy she possesses. Because of her lifelong thirst for God, I consider Tai Tai to be one of the greatest Christians I've ever known.

After I kissed my grandmother good night and went to bed, I couldn't fall asleep. I lay there thinking and praying, "Oh God, I want to desire you the way Tai Tai desires you. I want to experience the same holy passion for you that is so evident in her."

In the last chapter, I explained that one way to experience certainty in your relationship with God is to believe the promises God makes to sinners like you and me. Now I want to explore the second way you can experience certainty: through the presence of God in your life. So in this chapter I invite you to examine your feelings and desires for God. What do you love most? What are your heart's deepest longings?

When God becomes your most passionate desire, you will find growing certainty in life's most important relationship.

THE TEST OF THE HEART

Many people think that being a Christian is all about what we do or don't do, that it's all about how we act. And how we act and what we do are important. God, like any good father, wants obedient children who behave. But authentic Christians are not people who never sin. They are not people who are externally perfect. They are people internally passionate and on fire for God.

God is just as interested in our affections as he is in our

actions. That's why Jesus condemned the Pharisees for their obsessive—but heartless—religious activity.

So when my kids ask me, "Dad, what's a Christian?" I always answer, "A Christian is one who can say, 'As a deer pants for flowing streams, so pants my soul for you, O God. My soul thirsts for God' " (Psalm 42:1–2).

A Christian is someone who thirsts for God, longs for God more than he or she longs for anything else in this world, hungers for God more than he or she craves health, wealth, status, good looks, easy relationships, well-behaved kids, or a spouse. That's my Grandmother Tai Tai.

The moment God adopts us into his family, the Holy Spirit removes our heart of stone and gives us a heart of flesh so that we become a new creation (2 Corinthians 5:17). When I finally submitted my life to God, he radically changed my heart. I started to long for the spiritual things I had been running from, and I started running from the destructive things I used to long for. The things I wanted most changed drastically. I no longer wanted to spend time with the same people, in the same places, doing the same things. I *wanted* to be with Christians; I *wanted* to pray; I *wanted* to read my Bible; I *wanted* to be in worship on Sunday mornings with God's people. Now, God knows my behavior didn't change overnight, but I began loving the things God loves and hating the things God hates. I began to love God.

This is one of the earmarks of someone who truly has a relationship with God—love for God and the things he loves. If you want to know whether you really know God, examine your heart and see what you love. What you want is a surer test of who you are than what you do or don't do.

FEELINGS, NOT JUST FACTS

Knowing God, much as in any other relationship, involves feelings and not just facts. This is one of the most important things that separate those who know about God from those who know God. Remember from chapter 2 how I described my own childhood and youth, how I knew all kinds of facts about God but didn't really know him? I said that true relationship with God involves so much more than simply being able to recall certain truths about God.

I know many Bible scholars and theologians who have devoted their entire adult lives to the academic study of God and who possess more factual knowledge about God than most people, and yet their knowledge of God is cold and unfeeling. To them, God is a philosophical idea or proposition more than a living, relational Being. As John Piper says, "The devil himself thinks more true thoughts about God in one day than a saint does in a lifetime, and God is not honored by it. The problem with the devil is not his theology, but his desires."[1]

To be sure, all true Christians believe the facts about God, and they think about those facts. God equipped us with intellectual abilities, and he expects us to use them in our relationship with him. In fact, in my opinion many Christians don't think enough about God—a problem I will address later in this chapter. At the same time, I believe that those who know fewer facts about God but love him more are far better off than those who know more about him but do not love him. Factual knowledge does not lead to relationship with God. God wants more. He wants you to want him, desire him, and love him. He wants your feelings—and he wants them deep and real.

If your relationship with God is real, the Holy Spirit will be alive and well in you, producing a passionate hunger and thirst for God. When the Spirit resides in your heart, he revolutionizes the things you love. You will no longer yearn for the things of this world, but you will begin to long for the things of God. As J. C. Ryle says, "Sense of sin and deep hatred to it, faith in Christ and love to him, delight in holiness and longing after more of it, love to God's people and distaste for the things of this world—these are the signs and evidences which always accompany true conversion."[2]

DOES THINKING MATTER MORE THAN FEELING?

Can we really trust our feelings? The ancient Greek philosophers championed the notion that thinking is more trustworthy and reliable than feelings, a belief that continues to this day. After all, the argument goes, feelings come and feelings go, but reason is our anchor in the shifting sea of emotion. Some call this the primacy of the intellect.

Even many Christians believe that argument. I've always been attracted to serious thinkers, and most of my close friends and the people I hang out with emphasize thinking over feeling. In fact, many of my friends tend to be skeptical of Christians who express feelings for God. To them, how a Christian thinks is more important than how a Christian feels.

For at least two reasons, I think these friends and the ancient Greeks were wrong.

God redeems both our feelings and our thinking. A few years ago I had lunch with the well-known Bible teacher and theologian J. I. Packer. Before our lunch, I attended a frustrating meeting with people who were making some unwise decisions and, I felt, disregarding God. I was sad, mad, and in a sour mood when I sat down to eat with Dr. Packer. I began to vent my frustration regarding the meeting I had just come from. A few minutes later, however, I caught myself and apologized.

"I'm sorry, Dr. Packer. Please forgive me," I said. "I didn't mean to unleash my feelings on you like that."

"Don't apologize, Tullian," he replied. "Your feelings are Christian feelings."

His reply changed my thinking forever. What he meant was that, since I am a Christian, the Holy Spirit lives in me, and the Spirit is renewing and restoring everything about me, including my feelings. I didn't need to apologize for my feelings, Dr. Packer said, because my feelings on this particular matter were consistent with God's feelings.

As I mentioned in chapter 5, sin corrupts every part of us, including both our feelings and our thinking. Our thoughts are no more reliable than our feelings, just as our feelings are no more reliable than our thoughts. But when God adopts us as his children and we enter into relationship with him, he begins the process of purifying and transforming both our thoughts and our feelings.

Then, over time, as we keep in step with the Spirit in our lives, God's feelings and our feelings, God's likes and our likes, God's desires and our desires begin to overlap more and more. As we grow closer to God and our relationship with him deepens, our feelings become more reliable because they become more God-centered.

If you are a Christian, when you think rightly about God, it helps you feel rightly about God. But the reverse is also true: When you feel rightly about God, it also helps you to think rightly about God. True feelings inform true thoughts just as true thoughts inform true feelings. God wants us to experience our relationship to him with all of our parts, with the totality of our being. Therefore, Christians are to experience their relationship to God in the way they think *and* how they feel. They are to be people who think deeply about God *and* feel passionately for God. So putting a premium on thinking above feeling is philosophically Greek, not biblically Christian.

In fact, it's impossible to encounter the living God without emotion. In the poetry of the Psalms, God's people express emotional desperation and cries for deliverance, loud celebration and somber contemplation. Throughout Scripture we see people in the presence of God weeping over their sin, celebrating their forgiveness, exalting in God's bigness, and fearing God's wrath. People dance, fall down, cry out, and in many other ways express their desires and feelings for God.

A Christian's emotion for God, however, is to be grounded in God's truth. But some professing Christians today have moved beyond healthy God-centered emotion and into what I call *emotionalism*—feelings for feelings' sake. Turn on certain Christian television programs, and you will witness emotionalism in full display. There is little God-centered, biblical truth being taught, but there's plenty of emotional silliness. I suspect that emotionalism is what many of my serious-thinking buddies react against.

Just the other day I talked to a woman in my neighborhood who attends a church down the road. She explained how she thinks "following the Spirit's lead" is more important than reading the Bible and meditating on God's truth. As we talked more, it became clear that by "following the Spirit," she meant something like "going with your gut." That's emotionalism.

If your feelings for God aren't fueled by God's truth, then your feelings are leading you away from God and not toward him. If you can't identify a theological *why* behind your emotional *what,* then you can wonder if you've been snagged by emotionalism. Getting caught up in an emotional moment is no more proof that you're a child of God than getting caught up in an intellectual mood is. Both truthless emotionalism and emotionless intellectualism lead us astray. Neither of those roads will lead you to certainty in life's most important relationship.

AN UNTHINKING CHRISTIAN IS AN OXYMORON

So far in this chapter I've tried to show the importance of desires and feelings as they relate to our relationship with God. But I am in no way suggesting that thinking is unimportant. Earlier I said that too many Christians have bought into the Greek argument that thinking is more important than feelings, but the opposite is also true: far too many Christians believe that thinking is irrelevant. Many well-meaning Christians have adopted the mantra "Doctrine divides; love unites." As a result, serious study of God has fallen on hard times.

This is bad news. An unthinking Christian is an oxymoron. One way we identify God's presence in our lives is by the quality and seriousness of our thinking about God. What we think about God and how we think about him matters.

A gifted vocalist sang an old gospel tune on a Christian television program. After the song, the show's host walked on stage, clapping and shouting, "Thank you, brother, thank you. That was wonderful. Isn't Christianity wonderful? I mean, who cares whether it's true or not?"

That's ridiculous! If Christianity isn't true, if Jesus Christ didn't die on the cross for sinners and rise again, then a relationship with God isn't possible. And if a relationship with God isn't possible, then the answer to the question "Do I know God?" becomes a resounding no!

What we think about God matters. He commands us to love him with all our mind as well as with all our heart. As Christian philosopher Francis Schaeffer said, "Ideas have consequences." How we think affects how we feel and how we live. If our thinking is out of kilter, our feelings, desires, and lives will be out of kilter too. On the other hand, when we read the Bible and encounter God's holiness, goodness, love, sovereignty, bigness, and glory, our hearts ought to well up with raging emotion. F. W. Faber wrote, "Deep theology is the best fuel of devotion; it readily catches fire and once kindled it burns long."[3]

How could a true child of God encounter the infinite truth of God and not feel anything? I don't think it's possible.

EXAMINE YOUR HEART

J. C. Ryle said in his book *Practical Religion,* "If you would know whether your relationship with God is real, try it by the feelings toward Christ which it produces." So your feelings, loves, and desires speak volumes about your true relationship with God. When God adopts you into his eternal family and you begin to know him, your feelings will run deep as he increasingly becomes your greatest desire. When he adopts you into his family, he gives you a brand-new heart that begins to love what God loves and hate what he hates. You begin to long for God, desire God, hunger for God, experience joy in God, and exalt over God.

Do you want to know whether you know God? One way is to examine your heart. What do you love? What are your deepest desires? What do you feel toward God? If you truly have a relationship with him, your feelings will be real and passionate. He wants to develop you into someone who seeks to glorify him in the way you think and the way you feel. He wants your life marked by gravity and gladness, depth and delight, doctrine and devotion, precept and passion, truth and love (Matthew 22:37; John 4:23–24; 1 Corinthians 14:15; Ephesians 4:15).

Does this describe you? When you begin to love what God loves and hate what he hates, your life will bear the fruit of what you love and hate. And this leads us to the third way you can experience certainty in your relationship with God. When you are truly a child of God, your life will show evidence of your new relationship with him.

8

Outward Evidence of Inward Events

How does obedience to God
assure me of my salvation?

Faith that saves has one distinguishing quality:
saving faith is a faith that produces obedience;
it is a faith that brings about a new way of life.
—BILLY GRAHAM

Conner is one of the teenagers I love hanging out with. He's the youngest son in a wonderful Christian family who attends our church. At seventeen Conner is half my age, but he's full of life, loves to have fun, and is a blast to be around. We never have a dull moment when we're together. At the same time, he's always genuinely polite and respectful, and he's as comfortable with adults as he is with his peers. He's athletic, good-looking, and smart.

Even Conner's spiritual life seems grounded. He says he believes in Jesus, has no intellectual problems with the Christian faith, and believes it's the truth. He says he really likes God, and he quickly acknowledges that it was God who provided him with a good upbringing, good health, and every other good thing he has. He expresses deep gratitude for the life God gave him.

To most people who know him, Conner appears admirable in every way. But what most people don't know is that Conner struggles with doubt about his relationship with God. And probably with good reason.

Conner confesses that, despite his Christian beliefs, his interests and behavior are often not Christian. He enjoys doing things with his friends that he knows are wrong and do not honor God. He says he gets bored easily and needs constant entertainment. And since South Florida offers every pleasure under the sun, he finds himself continually pursuing fun through unwise and un-godly choices.

Conner knows what's right, yet he often chooses to live in a way that isn't right. And the tension in this conflict makes him wonder, *Do I really know God?*

I understand Conner's struggle. And I'm glad that spending eternity with God doesn't depend on my behavior, because for the most part I'm not well behaved. For some people, including my wife, compassion, putting others first, patience, generosity, and kindness seem to come naturally. For me, however, every day the pursuit of holiness is a fierce battle. I know what goes on inside my heart, and I know I'm not good enough to be God's friend or worthy of his eternal favor. I'm a self-centered, arrogant sinner who's more concerned about me than anyone else. Why, then, did God choose to adopt me? I have no idea. But I do know this: choosing me displays his amazing grace—because everyone who knows me knows that on my own I never would have chosen God. God adopts people like me into his family because of his grace, not because we could ever be good enough.

But while it's true that being good enough has nothing to do with establishing a relationship to God, it has everything to do with enjoying fellowship with God. Maybe this is really what's going on with Conner right now. Maybe he really does have a relationship with God, but he quit pursuing God to chase after a life he thinks will offer him more joy, and as a result he now questions his relationship with God.

As I explained in chapter 5, your good works can never be good enough to earn you a place in God's family. But if you are truly a child of God, your life will produce good works, and your good works will help reassure you that you really do know him. So this chapter is intended to help people like Conner understand how they can regain that sweet sense of relational closeness and security with God.

As the Bible says, "Make your calling and election sure" (2 Peter 1:10).

THE DIFFERENCE BETWEEN RELATIONSHIP
AND FELLOWSHIP

Throughout this book I've tried to show how you can know with certainty that you have an eternal relationship to God your Father. When I say "relationship to God," I mean your spiritual birth into God's family—the moment God saves you from your sins, adopts you as his child, and promises that you will spend eternity with him in heaven. The moment God adopts you, your relationship with him changes forever, from his being your rightful Judge to his being your royal Father.

Once you are a child of God, your relationship with him will never change. But your fellowship with him might.

When I say "fellowship with God," I mean that daily experience of God and his love that we enjoy when we speak to him in prayer and he speaks to us in the Bible. It is that daily experience of basking in God's special attention for us as his children. *Fellowship* simply describes how well we're getting along with our heavenly Father.

As we've already seen, getting *into* God's family depends on God alone. There's nothing you and I can do to earn our way into that family. But—and please notice the distinction—once we're in the family, getting *along* with our heavenly Father requires diligent effort on our part.

In his classic book *Basic Christianity*, John Stott describes the difference between relationship and fellowship like this:

Suppose a boy is offensively rude to his parents. A cloud descends on the home. There is tension in the atmosphere. Father and son are not on speaking terms. What has happened? Has the boy ceased to be a son? No. Their relationship has not changed; it is their fellowship which has been broken. Relationship depends on birth; fellowship depends on behavior. As soon as the boy apologizes, he is forgiven. And forgiveness restores fellowship. Meanwhile, his relationship has stayed the same. He may have been temporarily a disobedient, and even a defiant son; but he has not ceased to be a son. So it is with the children of God. When we sin, we do not forfeit our relationship to him as children, though our fellowship with him is spoiled until we confess and forsake our sin. As soon as we "confess our sin, he is faithful and just to forgive us our sin and cleanse us from all unrighteousness" (1 John 1:9).[1]

Allow me to explain the distinction between relationship and fellowship another way. Remember in chapter 2 when I described eternal security? When God adopts sinners into his family, he establishes a relationship with them that will last forever. No one can ever take that relationship away, and no matter what they do, no matter how badly they may fail in life, God will never abandon them. "I am sure that neither death nor life, nor angels nor rulers, nor things present nor things to come, nor powers, nor height nor depth, nor anything else in all creation, will be able to separate us from the love of God in Christ Jesus our Lord" (Romans 8:38–39).

I also explained the concept of assurance of salvation. Assurance of salvation is your inner awareness—or your sense—of your eternal security. That is, God promises that if you are a Christian, you will spend eternity with him, no matter what, and he wants you to know it (1 John 5:13). He wants you to feel the assurance and certainty that you are no longer a slave to sin but are now an adopted child of God. And it is your fellowship with God that will create in you the sense of relational security you long for. The stronger your fellowship with God is, the stronger your assurance of salvation will be. Your feelings of assurance don't change your eternal relationship with God one bit, but as Martyn Lloyd-Jones said, they are "essential to the *joy* of our salvation."

Marriage is a good example of what I mean. My wife, Kim, and I got married on July 8, 1994, starting a lifelong relationship. But just because we have a relationship as husband and wife doesn't mean that we always experience the joy of that relationship. Our relationship alone doesn't guarantee a good marriage. It's possible to live in a marriage relationship and feel miserable. Thankfully Kim and I enjoy our fellowship with each other, because it's something we work hard at. We go on vacations together. We regularly go out for dinner. We make time for each other and show interest in what the other is doing. It's only as we work at fellowship with each other that we enjoy the sense of relationship and security we have as husband and wife.

In the same way, when you pursue fellowship with God, when you "work out" your relationship with him, you will experience the sweet security and peace that comes when you *know* that you know God.

And how do we work out our relationship with God? The Bible says that we pursue fellowship with God by obeying him. Keep in mind that no amount of obedience can ever persuade God to adopt us into his family. But obedience does have a lot to do with our experience of fellowship with God and therefore our assurance of salvation.

FELLOWSHIP THROUGH OBEDIENCE

By obedience, I don't just mean determined, external compliance to God's rules. While obedience does involve keeping his commands, God wants more than mere rigid compliance to a set of dos and don'ts. Obedience that honors God flows from a heart that loves him and wants nothing more than to please him by doing everything he asks. In the Bible, love for God and obedience to God are two sides of the same coin. They are inseparable: "This is the love of God, that we keep his commandments" (1 John 5:3).

Jesus said, "Love the Lord your God with all your heart and with all your soul and with all your mind. This is the great and first commandment" (Matthew 22:37–38). Do you love God?

Your actions answer the question. Jesus said, "If you love me, you will keep my commandments" (John 14:15).

The New Testament letter of First John was written so people could know whether they have eternal life (1 John 5:13). God doesn't want any of his children going through life doubting their relationship with him. When people have a relationship with God, he wants them to know it. Throughout the letter John identifies three ways you can know whether you have eternal life: what you believe, what you love, and how you behave. In the last two chapters we looked at the first two ways you can know whether you have a relationship with God. Now let's look at the third way you can know: obedience to God.

John said plainly, "By this we know that we have come to know him, if we keep his commandments. Whoever says 'I know him' but does not keep his commandments is a liar, and the truth is not in him" (1 John 2:3–4). A few verses later he says practically the same thing: "Whoever keeps his commandments abides in him, and he in them. And by this we know that he abides in us, by the Spirit whom he has given us" (1 John 3:24).

In other words, God gives the Holy Spirit only to those who truly know him. And one of the ways we can know whether we have the Holy Spirit is when we're obeying God's commandments.

So John was clear. If you have no interest in obeying God, you can be fairly certain that you don't have the Holy Spirit. And if you don't have the Holy Spirit, then it's absolutely certain that you don't have a relationship with God. But if you *are* intent on obeying God, it's fairly certain the Holy Spirit lives in you, and you do have an eternal relationship with God.

As I've said before, when God adopts you into his family, he gives you a brand-new heart. And with that new heart, you will begin to delight in the law of God (Psalm 1:2). You will find yourself praying with the psalmist,

Open my eyes, that I may behold
wondrous things out of your law....
Your testimonies are my delight;
they are my counselors. (Psalm 119:18, 24—but see
the whole psalm)

If you are a true Christian, you understand that obedience to God isn't bondage. It's the passageway to true freedom and the powerful assurance that you are God's child forever.

The Perfect Problem

Now, before you put this book down utterly discouraged, you should know that obedience doesn't mean perfection. While John explained how important obedience is, he went on to say that we'll never be perfect: "If we say we have no sin, we deceive ourselves, and the truth is not in us" (1 John 1:8). Even as children of God, we'll continue to struggle against sin.

The apostle Paul agonized over ongoing sin. When God adopted Paul into his family, he planted within him new thoughts, new desires, and new behavior. Paul thought differently, felt differently, and lived differently. But at the same time, he discovered that when he wanted to do good, evil was right there with him. As a result, the good things he wanted to do he didn't do, and the bad things he didn't want to do he did. This fierce internal battle led him to cry out in desperation, "Wretched man that I am! Who will deliver me from this body of death?" (Romans 7:24).

I don't know about you, but that certainly describes my life. John Murray explains the problem: "It is one thing for the enemy to occupy the capital, it is another for his defeated hosts to harass the garrisons of the Kingdom."[2] Before God rescued us, sin was our ruler and it enjoyed governing our souls. God dethroned sin in our lives when he adopted us as children, but it continues to harass us with ruthless assaults.

In other words, even though we've been adopted into God's family and sin no longer controls us, sin still remains in us. And because of that, we'll never live perfectly obedient lives this side of heaven. But that day is coming! For all of us who have been forgiven our sins through Jesus Christ, the day is coming when we'll work and worship completely free of sin, with sinless hearts and minds in a new world, with no more pain, no more tears, no more disappointment, no more failure.

Until then, however, if you are a Christian, you'll battle imperfections and sin. But while you'll never live a perfectly obedient life, John made it clear that, as one of God's children, you will live differently than you did before.

DIFFERENT, NOT PERFECT

I recently talked to a woman who has been having serious problems with her husband. She professes to be a Christian, but the pain and frustrations of her marriage led her to seek affection from another man. She admitted to me that what she's doing is wrong, and she acknowledged that adultery is a sin and that God hates it. So why does she continue? "No one's perfect," she said.

To be fair, we all make excuses like that, justifying and rationalizing our sins and imperfections with something lame like "No one's perfect." I know, because I do it all the time. For example, I speed. I know it's wrong, but my driving record is horrible, because I love driving fast. When my wife is in the car with me, she gently lets me know I'm breaking the speed limit, and I typically respond, "I'm just keeping up with traffic, honey."

It's easy to deflect responsibility for our sins by finding comfort in "No one's perfect"—as if corruption in you excuses corruption in me. And the thing is, it *is* true—nobody is perfect. But if you're serious about answering the question "Do I know God?" you won't find much comfort in that tired excuse. Why? Because when God establishes a relationship with you, the Spirit of God produces in you the desire to live differently. You begin to experience God-honoring thoughts and feelings, and that leads to God-honoring behavior. And you not only change internally (which is what I talked about in the last chapter), but those internal changes also lead to genuine changes in your daily life.

Jesus said that all true children of God will be known by their fruit. And Paul later identified this fruit as "love, joy, peace, patience, kindness, goodness, faithfulness, gentleness, self-control" (Galatians 5:22–23). As a child of God, you begin to say no to temptations you used to say yes to. You start thinking about the way you speak, the things you do, and the way you live. You care about how God wants you to act. You start pursuing a lifestyle that you know will honor God.

One of the reasons I'm certain I know God is that how I live now compared to how I used to live is radically different. Trust me, those who know me best will tell you that I'm far from perfect. But those same people will also tell you that I'm radically different from the way I used to be. My behavior tells quite a different story than it used to: the way I now live on the outside points to the spiritual changes God has made inside me.

Jim and Sherry, a couple in our church, are another example of this change. Before God saved them, they were unmarried and living together, which they never thought was a big deal. But when God adopted them into his family, they started reading the Bible, and they learned about God's commands regarding sex and marriage. They began to understand that sleeping together was wrong, so Jim decided they needed to make a change. At first Jim simply tried sleeping on the couch. That lasted about forty-eight hours. So Jim and Sherry wondered whether he should move out altogether.

It wasn't an easy decision. Everything from the mortgage to the phone bill was in both of their names. Neither of them earned enough money for a second place. They loved each other and planned to get married one day, but they also knew that they needed time to grow in their new relationships with God before they got married. So Jim packed up his stuff and moved in with his mother. He was in his forties at the time, and his mother didn't live near where he worked. It was terribly inconvenient. But that didn't matter to him. He was serious about his relationship with God, and he was serious about obeying him. According to both Jim and Sherry, this difficult decision led them to a sweeter assurance of God's presence than they had known before. They've been married now for many years, and both of them point to that difficult, God-honoring decision as a turning point in their relationship.

The missionary Henry Martyn experienced a similar change in his life when God adopted him. "The work is real," he said. "I can no more doubt it than I can my own existence. The whole current of my desires is altered; I am walking quite another way, though I am incessantly stumbling in that way."[3]

So while those of us who are Christians are not yet what we will one day be, we are no longer what we used to be. We're like the Israelites during their wilderness wanderings in Sinai—while we've been rescued from slavery in Egypt, we haven't yet entered the Promised Land.

LOOKING FOR GROWTH

When God saves us, he intends for us to grow. So one of the surest ways to tell whether God has saved you is to examine your life and determine whether you are growing. Is the Spirit producing a life of obedience in you? Is your life different than it used to be? Are you moving toward God or away from God? Your pursuit of holiness and practice of godliness are sure signs that you belong to God.

God urges us to "make every effort to supplement [our] faith with virtue, and virtue with knowledge, and knowledge with self-control, and self-control with steadfastness, and steadfastness with godliness, and godliness with brotherly affection, and brotherly affection with love." And as we do so, he promises it will keep us "from being ineffective or unfruitful in the knowledge of our Lord Jesus Christ" (2 Peter 1:5–8).

In other words, as we obey God and put into practice the new life he has given us, we make our "calling and election sure" (2 Peter 1:10). That is, the more we live in ways that please God, the more we'll enjoy close fellowship with him. And the closer our fellowship with God, the more we'll experience the warm inner assurance and certainty that we are children of God.

At the same time, disobedience and sin can rob us of our fellowship with God and even lead us to question our relationship to him. Remember Conner?

The same thing that happened to Conner happened to me in college as I was preparing to be a preacher. As I got busier with schoolwork, I slowly began neglecting the spiritual disciplines in my life. My prayer life became spotty, I read my Bible less, and I allowed sinful behaviors to creep back into my life. I had been a Christian for almost two years, but suddenly I felt like my relationship with God was sinking, and I didn't know why. I went for a drive one afternoon, and I began to wonder, *Is my relationship with God real?* After all, when I compared my life to the way Christians acted in the Bible, I didn't see many similarities. My disobedience had robbed me of that inner sense of relationship with God, and once again I felt uncertain of who I was. What had happened? Had I lost my relationship to God?

No! Once God adopts us into his family, that relationship is forever. Nothing we do can ever change our eternal relationship with God. But what we do can change our fellowship with him. When I stopped obeying God and started acting in ways that did not honor him, I didn't lose my place in the family; I lost my fellowship with God, and I lost my inner assurance about my relationship with him.

If you want to feel secure in your relationship to God, then continue to pursue God by living the way you know he wants you to live. The harder you pursue God in your thinking, feeling, and living, the more inner awareness you'll experience. And the softer you pursue God in your thinking, feeling, and living, the less inner awareness you'll experience. When you sin, God will not remove you from his family, but your sin will keep you from genuine fellowship, the experience of God's loving presence in your life.

We "cannot experience high levels of assurance while [we] participate in low levels of obedience," Joel Beeke wrote. That's why Paul stressed our need to fight the good fight, press on, strain forward, and run the race. That's why the Bible has so much to say about how we, as children of God, are to live. We have to put off old sinful habits and put on new godly habits (Ephesians 4:20–24).

During that season in college when I lost the sweet inner awareness that I was God's child, I examined how I was living. God helped me see that my pursuit of him had grown weak. I wanted that sense of God's love again, so I confessed that he had become secondary in my life and that I needed him to be first again. Then I strengthened my pursuit of God, spending more time with him in prayer and Bible study, and I grew more determined to make sure sin could not negotiate with my soul.

As I obeyed God more, I soon recovered my sense of God's relationship, and he reminded me that, even though I had felt separated from him because of my sin, he had never been far away. He reminded me that he would never leave me nor forsake me (Hebrews 13:5), that his capacity to forgive is far greater than my capacity to sin, and that his pursuit of me is far stronger than my ability to run.

RETROSPECTION, INTROSPECTION, AND EXTROSPECTION

Over the past three chapters, I've shown you three ways that you can *know* you know God: when you believe in his promises, when you love what he loves and hate what he hates, and when your life shows the outward evidence of the living faith inside you.

Another helpful way to put this is that if you want to know whether or not you have a relationship to God, it involves retrospection, introspection, and extrospection.

By retrospection, I mean looking back and remembering the relational promises of God that we examined in chapter 6. This involves your thinking capacities because it has to do with believing. It takes careful thought to properly evaluate the relational promises that God makes to sinners and to believe them. Unlike various Eastern religions that encourage the disengagement of the mind, knowing God demands strong intellectual engagement. I'm not saying you have to be an intellectual to be a child of God. I simply mean there is no way any of us can truly know God if we check our minds at the door. Serious, thoughtful inquiry into the eternal promises that God lays out in the Bible will help all of us attain a fuller assurance of our salvation.

By introspection, I mean looking in and examining God's presence in your life, a presence we defined in chapter 7. Is God the object of your most passionate desires? Do you love what God loves and hate what God hates? Do you long for God, hunger for God, thirst for God? This inevitably involves your emotional capacities because it has to do with feeling. Obviously, because our feelings are tainted with sin, our desires will always be somewhat of a mixed bag. Sometimes we will feel God, and other times we won't. Sometimes we will desire God, and other times we won't. The real question is whether we want to desire God or not. I find myself praying on a regular basis, "O God, help me to want to want you." That's the real issue. If we have no feelings for God whatsoever, then it's safe to say that we don't know him.

And by extrospection, I mean looking out and observing the external production of God in your life. This involves your volitional capacities because it has to do with obedience. Do you seek to obey God? Do you love others? Do the patterns of your life indicate movement toward the will of God or movement away from the will of God? Are you working hard, by God's grace and with God's power, to do what pleases God?

Now let's look at some practical spiritual disciplines that will help you make these three ways of knowing that you know God a growing part of your daily life.

9

The Practical Pursuit of Assurance

What can I do to experience the assurance
of my salvation?

Grow in the grace and knowledge
of our Lord and Savior Jesus Christ.
—APOSTLE PETER (2 PETER 3:18)

Think about the important relationships in your life—your
spouse, your children, your parents, your closest friends.
Every good, healthy relationship requires loving effort. In the previous chapter, for example, I explained how my wife and I love
each other, but to maintain our love, we make time for each
other, engage each other, and listen to each other. Sometimes it

feels like we're living on a fast-moving treadmill. Remembering and protecting what's really important takes effort. But we don't want to take our love or our relationship for granted, so we carefully and intentionally plan and prepare for the time we spend together, making sure we don't miss opportunities to enjoy each other. After all, true love takes work. As contradictory as it may sound, enduring passion requires discipline.

Yesterday a man told me how his relationship with his wife had grown cold. "I don't know what happened," he said. "It seems like only yesterday that my wife and I were so close. We enjoyed the same things. We enjoyed the same people. We had so much in common. But now we seem so far apart."

As we talked, it became clear that they had started drifting apart after their first child was born. Their lives grew busier. Work demanded more of his time, and the new baby demanded more of hers. She started going to bed earlier so she could feed the baby in the wee hours of the night, and that meant she and her husband rarely went to bed together. They spent less and less time together, just the two of them. Their conversations grew shorter and more task focused. Slowly they grew apart.

Before the baby came, they found spending time with each other easy. But afterward, spending time with each other required discipline—and they didn't have it. They naively thought that healthy relationships just happen.

The same is true of our relationship with God. If you are a child of God, he wants a healthy relationship with you. He wants you to know and experience how much he loves you. But if you want that kind of healthy relationship with God, if you want to experience his love and nearness, if you want to *know* that you know God, it will require work and spiritual discipline. As the apostle James wrote, "Draw near to God, and he will draw near to you" (James 4:8).

In this chapter I want to look at practical ways you and I can draw near to God so we can experience God's nearness to us as his adopted children.[1]

ARENAS OF GRACE

Spiritual disciplines are designed to draw fallen, fickle humans (that's you and me) into God's presence. They are intentional practices that create the space we need to encounter God and experience his nearness. And God has graciously provided his children with places to meet him—rendezvous points, if you will. T. M. Moore calls these rendezvous points "special arenas of grace." It is in these arenas where we experience the intensity of God's love and care for us. It is in these arenas where our love for God and God's love for us are renewed and deepened.

Spiritual disciplines, by the way, do not guarantee us a life without trials. We're broken sinners living in a broken world, and the spiritual disciplines I describe below are not magic formulas that protect us against defeat and discouragement. We'll still face seasons when we feel alone and desperate, and we'll experience disappointment when we fail in our attempts to pursue God. But as Moore said, spiritual disciplines help us both to grow in our relationship with God and to deal with the "difficulties and trials of life."[2] And if we ignore them, we'll find ourselves spiritually famished, drifting from God much as my friend found himself drifting from his wife. In many ways, then, a healthy relationship with God depends on you and me meeting with God in these places—these arenas of grace. Where is it, then, that we meet with God? Where are those places where we can experience the intensity of God's love for us?

Author Donald Whitney lists ten spiritual disciplines: Bible reading, prayer, worship, evangelism, serving, stewardship, fasting, silence and solitude, journaling, and learning. All of these are biblically based practices that have enriched the Christian tradition for two thousand years. As we incorporate these disciplines into our lives, our experience of God will surely run high and hot. They're all important and valuable. But for our purposes here, I want to highlight what I consider the three foundational spiritual practices: Bible reading, prayer, and commitment to the church.

GOD-BREATHED READING

My five-year-old daughter, Genna, sings a song that goes like this:

> Read your Bible and pray every day, pray every day,
>   pray every day.
> Read your Bible and pray every day, and you'll grow,
>   grow, grow.

As simple as the song is, it contains the secret of Christian growth. It's the first part of the song—"read your Bible"—that I want to examine first.

Our relationship to God cannot grow and thrive apart from reading the Bible and hearing it taught. The Bible is where God personally speaks to us. In 2 Timothy 3:16–17 Paul wrote, "All Scripture is breathed out by God and profitable for teaching, for reproof, for correction, and for training in righteousness, that the man of God may be competent, equipped for every good work."

In the Bible, God tells us who he is, who we are, and how we are to live. It's where God encourages us, corrects us, challenges us, comforts us, and exhorts us. It's where he offers Fatherly protection, warning his children about enemy territory and showing us how to avoid the devil's land mines. And it's where he gives us the power we need to press on and strain forward.

As we read the Bible and hear it taught, we encounter God's love and affection for his adopted children. We encounter God's promise that, for the children of God, the best is yet to come. God tells us in his Word that he will forgive our past, empower our present, and perfect our future. It's when we hear God speak these truths to us in the Bible that we begin to experience the assurance of salvation.

If you're unfamiliar with the Bible and don't know where to begin reading, or if reading the Bible intimidates you because it's hard to understand, let me offer some help.

First, get yourself a Bible-reading plan. I confess that if I don't have a plan, I don't read—plain and simple. I need direction, a plan that tells me what to read and when. Two resources have helped me a lot. The first is the *Discipleship Journal* Bible Reading Plan.[3] This plan gives four passages to read every day of the year. What I usually do is read two of the passages in the morning and two at night. Do this for one year, and you'll make it all the way through the Bible.

The second resource I use is *The One Year Bible*. Like the *Discipleship Journal* plan, this one also designates passages to read every day of the year. But I use this tool a little differently from the other one. Instead of reading all the passages each day, I usually read just two of the passages every day for one year and then the other two passages every day the second year. So, for me, *The*

One Year Bible really turns into *The Two Year Bible.* That's fine. The Bible never tells us how much we have to read in a given day.

If you have trouble understanding the Bible when you read it, I also recommend that you get a good study Bible. A study Bible adds helpful notes and explanations to the full text of God's Word. In my opinion the best one is the *Spirit of the Reformation Study Bible,* published by Zondervan. It provides excellent notes and articles on difficult-to-understand passages and concepts in the Bible.

Whether you choose to use a study Bible or not, the important thing is to discipline yourself every day to read your Bible even if you don't understand everything you read. That's right. Whether you understand everything or not, setting aside time every day to read the Bible means you're serious about spending time with God, and he honors that. Your relationship with God is sure to grow if you give him time.

When my older son, Gabe, was just learning to talk, he gabbed a mile a minute. Most of the time we couldn't understand a word he said. But just the act of him talking—and us listening—truly enhanced our relationship. It was valuable communication even if we didn't always understand. That early season in his life knitted us together in acceptance, listening, love, and laughter.

Don't underestimate God's ability to nourish your relationship with him as he speaks to you in the Bible, even if you don't understand everything he says. Discipline yourself to listen to God, and you will grow, grow, grow.

PRAYER—A CONVERSATION WITH GOD

The second part of my daughter's song is "pray every day." I often tell the people at New City Church, "The Bible is God's way of speaking to us, and prayer is our way of speaking to God." Every healthy relationship requires regular two-way conversation. In the same way, Bible reading without prayer is not enough, just as prayer without Bible reading is not enough. The most effective way to experience God's nearness in your life is to wed the two; enjoy the two-way conversation that God offers. Practically, this happens as you read your Bible and then turn what you have read into prayer.

Essentially, prayer is conversation with God. When God adopts us into his family, it is as much a part of our new nature to pray as it is the nature of a child to cry. One sure sign you know God, then, is that you talk to him—and want to. A prayerless life is a godless life.

As I said in chapter 7, a Christian is someone who longs for God more than he or she longs for anything else in this world. And one of the main ways this longing for God expresses itself is through prayer. When we pray, we expose our hearts to our heavenly Father, hiding nothing from him. In prayer we express our adoration for God and bring our requests before him. In prayer we confess our sins to God and offer him thanksgiving for who he is and what he's done.

"What a man is on his knees, that he is and nothing more," said Robert Murray McCheyne. When we pray, we bring all that we are to all that he is, trusting that he never turns a deaf ear to his talking children. God is the ultimate listener. He never promises to give us everything we want. But he does promise to listen and give us everything we need. Being the perfect Father, he promises to give good things to those who ask him (Matthew 7:11).

Without a doubt, prayer isn't always easy. In fact, at times, prayer can be a real struggle. I struggle with prayer myself, and honestly I've never met a Christian who hasn't. The good news, though, is that God promised to help us pray. When we find ourselves lacking both energy and words, God promises to motivate us, animate us, and carry us.

> The Spirit helps us in our weakness. For we do not know what to pray for as we ought, but the Spirit himself intercedes for us with groanings too deep for words. And he who searches hearts knows what is the mind of the Spirit, because the Spirit intercedes for the saints according to the will of God. (Romans 8:26–27)

I remember one of my professors in seminary saying, "This means that when we are weak, God speaks to God through us." Amazing nearness!

I'm often asked whether it's necessary to set aside a special time and place to pray every day for extended periods of time or whether it's enough to "pray as you go," so to speak—praying in the car, praying at the ball field, praying as you work out. I always answer this question with an analogy from my marriage.

There are times when my wife and I talk "as we go": when she's cooking dinner, when we're helping the kids with homework, when we're watching my son's basketball game. And that's good. There's nothing wrong with small talk. Any relationship that lacks small talk is an unhealthy relationship. But if small talk were the only conversation we had with each other, our relationship would suffer. I love those special times when we take long walks on the beach, when just the two of us are out to dinner, when we spend time together at night after the kids are in bed. That's when we engage each other in a deeper, more intentional way; it's when we talk about the big things going on in our lives. When we combine casual conversation with deeper conversation, we nurture and enjoy each other more, and our love for each other grows stronger.

The same is true when it comes to our relationship with God. Certainly it's right and good to stay in touch with God as we move about the day. We are, after all, to "pray without ceasing"

(1 Thessalonians 5:17). But when we fail to combine casual conversation with deeper conversation, our relationship with God suffers. In my case, I use the morning hours to have those deeper, more concentrated conversations with God.

One of the best ways I've discovered to kick-start a healthier prayer life is to pray through Psalms. The psalms are really just prayers in poetic form. So when we use them, they not only teach us how to pray but also what to pray. And because the psalms are God's inspired words to us, when we pray through them, we cover subjects and emotions that God considers important.

Another resource I find tremendously helpful is a Puritan prayer book called *The Valley of Vision*. It's a collection of prayers that I often use when I can't think of anything to pray. They are deep, rich, and probing. I can't tell you how many times I've prayed through one of these prayers and thought, *That's exactly what I wanted to say to God. That's exactly what I* needed *to say to God.*

THE LIVING COMMUNITY

Commitment to the church is a spiritual discipline? I know it sounds unconventional, but let me explain what I mean.

When God saves us, he saves us as individuals, but he saves us *into* a community—the church, the living community of faith. This means there's no such thing as individualistic Christianity.

God never intended us to live our lives pursuing him on our own. After creating the world and pronouncing it all "very good" (Genesis 1:31), God said that one thing was not good. Speaking of Adam—and in a sense of each of us—he said, "It is not good that the man should be alone" (Genesis 2:18). While it's true that God is all we need, he wants us to enjoy his goodness and love through others.

Candidly, I just finished the hardest month of my life. At least it feels that way to me now. I can't remember another time when I felt so weak, so desperate, so in need of God to carry me. As I talked to my wife the other morning about this difficult month, I told her, "I'd like to say that because everything's been so hard, I've spent more time praying and poring over God's Word than I ever have before. I'd like to say that over the past month I've sought God harder than ever before." But the truth is, I didn't. I was so emotionally and spiritually drained that most days I just wanted to quit.

The one thing that got me through the past month, however, was that I depended heavily on my Christian brothers and sisters. Every day it seemed like God himself carried me on his back *through* the love and support of my church. In fact, this past Sunday I told them as much in my sermon. I said that I understand once more that to depend on God's people is to depend on God and vice versa.

The fact is, I can't follow God on my own, and neither can

you. We need each other; we need the church. The church is God's family, and as we experience love and grace in God's family, we also experience God's love and grace through them. When the church helps us and encourages us, it's God helping us and encouraging us through our brothers and sisters.

But experiencing God through his church takes work and discipline. It takes time. We experience God's devotion to us only as we devote ourselves to the church and invest in the people of God. Just as with any other spiritual discipline, however, the more we invest ourselves, the more deeply we'll experience God's assurance of his eternal love for us. The church is the communal arena of grace where God grows us, matures us, and changes us through one another. That's why it's simply not possible to know that you know God apart from the church.

My friend Joshua Harris wrote an impassioned book called *Stop Dating the Church,* which is a clear call to fall in love with the family of God. In that book he points out that one of the most practical ways to experience assurance of your salvation is to join a local church, because "the local church is the place where our new life in Christ is lived out and proven."

Sadly, not any local church will do. Some churches will help you in your spiritual journey; some won't. I often tell people that selecting a good church is one of the most important choices you will ever make. Check out chapter 5 of Josh's book for a helpful list of how to choose a good church.

Of course, since churches are made up of people in various stages of maturity, there's no such thing as a perfect church. If you hold out for a church that fits every criterion on your long list of preferences, you'll never engage. And that reminds me of a favorite story.

A few years ago I was in Starbucks with our music director, Brandon. As we waited in line to get our afternoon caffeine kick, the young barista behind the counter overheard us talking about our church, which at that point was only a year old, and we started chatting. Brandon soon invited her to visit our church one Sunday. She responded in typical postmodern fashion, saying, "I'm into spirituality, but I'm not really into organized religion."

Brandon, who has a wonderfully quick wit, replied, "Don't worry, we're really not that organized."

The barista's statement illustrates what many people believe today, namely that they can have a meaningful relationship with God without being connected to a local church. But it's just not possible to have Christ the head without Christ the body—his church (Ephesians 1:22–23; Colossians 1:18). The two are inseparable. To neglect the body of Christ is to neglect Christ. Just as no one can survive without air, so Christians can't survive without the church.

The bottom line is this: a real relationship with God will show itself in a real relationship with his people. And as we live our lives in the family of God, and as we listen to God through his Word and pray to him, God assures us of our salvation.

SEASONS OF DARKNESS

But even when we seek God with all our heart, strength, mind, and soul through the spiritual disciplines I've just described—praying, reading God's Word, and being committed to his church—we sometimes experience seasons of spiritual darkness and distance that are hard to understand. How can we hold on to God's assurance of his eternal love when all we experience of him is his absence?

In the next chapter let's examine one of the deepest mysteries of our Christian experience.

Knowing God in the Dark Night

How can I be assured of God's presence
when what I feel most is his absence?

The Christian must trust in a withdrawing God.
—WILLIAM GURNALL

Throughout this book I've tried to explain that if you have a relationship to God, he wants you to know it with absolute certainty. Cognitively, we enjoy this certainty as we know, believe, and act upon the truth of God's character and Word. Experientially, we enjoy this certainty as we pursue God, obey him, and draw nearer to him through important spiritual practices. In fact, the more we pursue God in our thinking, feeling, and doing, the more we experience God's assurance that we are his children forever.

But what if we are pursuing God in our thinking, feeling, and doing, and he still seems distant? What about those seasons in life when we draw near to God, but he doesn't draw near to us, at least as far as we can tell? Sometimes, no matter how much we love God and seek to honor him with our lives, it seems as if God disappears, and our souls grow cold in the awful silence.

My friend Larry understands that awful silence well. It came upon him when he was in his final year at a Christian college in Oregon, studying journalism. God gave him a passion for words and communication, and he looked forward to graduating in a few months and launching his career as a Christian writer and editor. He prayed regularly, studied the Bible, and attended chapel like most students at Christian colleges. God seemed present and everywhere. But one evening as he sat studying in his room, everything changed.

"It happened instantly," he says. "One moment I felt absolutely normal, safe and secure, close to God, and a second later it felt as if someone had turned off the light switch. I literally sat straight up, looking around the room to see what had happened. It's hard to explain, but I knew right then that God was gone. That's how it felt. God had left the room."

He felt abandoned and confused. Why did God leave? What

did Larry do that caused God to cast him aside? Didn't God promise never to leave him or forsake him?

Over the next several months, Larry prayed, fasted, confessed his sins, pored over his Bible, and pleaded for God to return—or at least to help him understand. But he experienced only silence. Many days he broke down weeping, confused and seemingly alone. "I've lived most of my life as a single man," he says, "but I've never experienced loneliness like that."

As the months passed, Larry became spiritually exhausted, and he felt his faith challenged and threatened. But he refused to let go, refused to quit pursuing God. One afternoon the following summer, after graduation, he finally collapsed to his knees at his parents' home.

"I was so emotionally and spiritually tired," he recalls. "I had prayed every prayer I could think of. I confessed and repented of every known sin. I just didn't have anything left to pursue God further. As tears rolled down my face, I decided to turn to God one more time: 'God, I don't know what to pray anymore. I committed my whole life to serve and worship you, but I don't know what that means now or if it even makes sense anymore. Everything I thought I knew about you—I don't know if it's true. I feel stripped and naked, and this is what's left: either you really don't exist and I've committed my life to a lie...or you really do exist and I have no idea who you truly are."

Just then, for the first time in eight months, Larry felt God smile. He sensed God saying, "Child, you *finally* understand. I'm here, and you're right—you have no idea who I really am. I am so much more than all the structures and boxes and bullet points you limited me to."

In that moment Larry sensed God picking him up out of darkness. That day he came to know God in a way that utterly changed his life. It was, according to Larry, a Job-like moment:

> I had heard of you by the hearing of the ear,
>> but now my eye sees you. (Job 42:5)

Eventually most Christians experience an awful season when God seems silent, remote, or missing altogether. If God is just an idea or force to you, like gravity, then this predicament might not sound so bad. But for Christians—those of us who know the reality of a personal relationship with God through Jesus Christ—the experience is calamitous.

What explains this unexpected turn of events? Sometimes God's distance is because of a sin we've committed or because we've neglected spending time with him. Those times are painful, but at least we understand why we no longer are experiencing his presence. And we know what to do to restore our fellowship with him: "If we confess our sins, he is faithful and just to forgive us our sins and to cleanse us from all unrighteousness" (1 John 1:9).

But what about those times when God seems to disappear, and we *are* pursuing him, we *are* spending time with him, we *are* obeying him, and we *have* confessed our sins? That's when we can cry out with the psalmist, "How long, O LORD? Will you forget me forever?" (Psalm 13:1) and "My God, my God, why have you forsaken me?" (Psalm 22:1). That's when many of us begin to wonder, *Do I really know God?*

Throughout history Christians have described these seasons of God's silence in various ways. Perhaps the most familiar phrase comes from the sixteenth-century Roman Catholic mystic Saint John of the Cross, who described these seasons as "the dark night of the soul"—that internal darkness that fills our hearts when it feels as though God has abandoned us. The Puritans described these periods as "God's dreadful withdrawal," when God seems strangely absent. They believed that to lose the awareness of God's presence is one of the worst things a child of God can face.

Even the Bible tells stories of men who experienced God's absence. After Job lost everything in his life, he asked God why. Read Job 30:15–22. Job isn't asking God why he lost everything; he's asking God, "Why have you left me?" There it is—God's dreadful withdrawal.

Dark nights like these can cause Christians to feel as if God has really abandoned us. We can begin to doubt whether we are saved.

But such seasons of darkness don't have to cause you to doubt your relationship to God. In fact, I want to show you how these seasons can have the opposite effect. God's dreadful withdrawal can actually be a comforting ache that assures you of your relationship to God.

THE COMFORT OF ACHE

When I was in seminary, my wife sometimes took our two small boys to spend a three-day weekend with her parents, who lived a few hours away. Because of school, I was rarely able to go with them. The first night by myself was always fun. I usually met some friends for dinner and a movie. For a few hours, I felt the relief of having fewer responsibilities, and I enjoyed coming and going as I pleased.

But the first morning after they left, when I would wake up to a silent house, it was hard. I missed hearing little feet and high voices first thing in the morning. I missed waking up to the adorable sound of Gabe and Nate playing with their *Star Wars* action figures. And I missed my wife calling us down to breakfast as the entire house filled with the aroma of freshly brewed coffee. All that relational activity made our house feel like a home. When they were gone, our home felt more like a cold shelter.

I still hate being away from my wife and kids. We don't travel without each other much these days, but when we do, I miss them terribly. When I have to leave my family for more than a day, I begin to experience an ache that ends only when I get back with them.

But when I'm away from my family and I feel that terrible sadness, I don't conclude that my relationship with them has been lost. In fact, I feel just the opposite. My sadness actually confirms the relationship. If I didn't miss them, if I didn't ache to get back to them, it would mean I don't really care about them and probably don't love them. So, ironically, the ache I experience when I'm apart from my family affirms my love for them. It's a sweet pain that makes my love feel alive and well, and it reminds me of just how much I need them. I guess the old adage really is true: absence makes the heart grow fonder.

The same is true of our relationship to God. As I said before, the Bible is full of stories about God's withdrawing from his people. I already mentioned Job. You can also find the experience in just about every psalm of lament.[1]

In Psalm 42, for example, the psalmist cried out to God because he was spiritually worn out and dried up. He knew that God alone offered the rest he needed and the water he craved. So he turned to God in his moment of spiritual desperation. But even though he turned to God, he lamented the fact that God seemed so far away. It's as if God had turned his back on the psalmist. So the psalmist cried out, "When shall I come and appear before God?" (verse 2).

He couldn't understand why God had seemingly concealed himself, and he felt isolated and alone.

My tears have been my food
    day and night,
while they say to me continually,
    "Where is your God?" (verse 3)

In his grief he romanticized the past:

These things I remember,
    as I pour out my soul:
how I would go with the throng
    and lead them in procession to the house of God
with glad shouts and songs of praise,
    a multitude keeping festival. (verse 4)

He remembered when God was near. He remembered the day when God's presence was strong and tangible.

He wanted to experience God again. He wanted to feel God's closeness again, and he couldn't understand why God chose to remain silent. He felt forgotten:

I say to God, my rock:
    "Why have you forgotten me?

Why do I go mourning
    because of the oppression of the enemy?"
        (verse 9)

One of the interesting things about this psalm is that, even though the psalmist felt the pain of God's dreadful withdrawal, he never doubted his relationship to God or questioned whether he knew God. Even though he felt God's distance, he continued to call him "my salvation and my God" (verses 5–6, 11). In fact, as he continued to write, the psalmist's hunger for God and his hope in God increased.

How could this be? How could the psalmist remain sure about his relationship to God even when God seemed to ignore him? What was his secret?

I think it's because he knew that if he had no relationship to God, then he wouldn't ache the way he did. That sort of ache assured him, as it should us, that he belonged to God. It assured him that the Holy Spirit lived in him and made him long for God. His ache did not make him doubt his love for God; it affirmed his love for God.

So when it seems as though God disappears from your life, the pain of his absence can actually revive and renew your love for him. The ache you feel is not a sign that he has abandoned you or that you don't really have a relationship with him; it should remind you of how much you love God, need God, and want God. Think about it: if you didn't know him, you wouldn't ache for him.

In fact, when God seems to withdraw from us, it's a gracious act of love. When God withdraws, it causes us to desire him more, to cry out to him, and to seek him in deeper ways than we ever did before. As psychologist Larry Crabb said, God wants to "increase our passion for knowing him until it is stronger than all other passions." Developing that passion in us, according to Crabb, "is a long difficult process to which God is relentlessly committed" because he loves us and wants what's best for us.[2] And what's best for us? God. That's why the Puritans said, "Desertions are not the interruptions of God's love, they are rather the act of God's love."[3]

LEARNING TO TRUST WHEN YOU CANNOT TRACE

What it boils down to is whether you trust God. The author of Psalm 42 did. As he reflected on his life, remembering all the dark valleys he had walked through, he recognized that God had never left him.

> My soul is cast down within me;
>   therefore I remember you
> from the land of Jordan and of Hermon,
>   from Mount Mizar. (Psalm 42:6)

Like David in Psalm 23, we can assume the psalmist trusted that,

> Even though I walk through the valley of the shadow of death,
>   I will fear no evil,
> for you are with me. (verse 4)

No matter how dark the circumstances of our lives become, no matter how distant God might seem, he always has our best interests at heart. Of course, believing this requires trust. No matter how well we live our Christian life, circumstances will not always turn out the way we want. Loved ones will still die; disease will still ravage friends; teenagers will still rebel; spouses will still leave; investments will still go bad; people will still cut us off in traffic. But despite it all, we can still trust that God is good and that he's committed to working all things out for our good.

C. S. Lewis said that trusting God is like taking a walk on the beach and looking out over the ocean: there's far more that you can't see than you can see. Whether you understand everything God is doing or not, he's trustworthy. And if you don't believe that, the time will come when you will lie down and quit, especially during the dark night of the soul. Faith is trusting God even when you cannot trace God. It is believing that no matter what you're going through, God is for you.

I remember experiencing God's dreadful withdrawal. It was

painful, and I was confused. I ached for God's nearness again, but it seemed like no matter what I did, God stayed hidden from me. In desperation I finally cried out to God, like Job, pleading with him to explain why he had seemingly left me.

Driving around one night, I started listening to a sermon on the radio. At the end of the sermon, the preacher said, "If you don't go to your grave in confusion, you won't go to your grave trusting. Explanations are a substitute for trust." I pulled over and started to cry. Like the psalmist of Psalm 42, I started remembering everything God had done for me throughout my life. I remembered how he chose me before the foundation of the world and how he brought me into an eternal relationship with himself. I remembered how he's blessed me with good health, a faithful wife, and three beautiful children. I remembered how, though I've never been rich, God has provided for all my material needs. I remembered the incredible privilege he has given me to share the gospel of Jesus Christ.

I cried, and I couldn't stop. It was as though God whispered in my ear, "Do you trust me? Have I ever let you down? Do you see how my timing has always been perfect? Trust me. I love you. I love you so much that I sent my Son to die on a cross for your sins so I could adopt you into my family forever."

When I remember that night—the time when God returned to remind me that he had never left—it still brings me to tears.

Trust God. Jesus promised that he would stay with you forever, that he would never leave nor forsake you. You may not always feel his presence, but God *is* always present. He promised. And no matter how you feel, he is always closer than you can imagine.

WAITING ON GOD

In our fast-paced, highly mobile, technologically driven world, the hardest thing to do is to "be still before the LORD and wait patiently for him" (Psalm 37:7). We want everything now. We want comfort now, convenience now, relief now. I have a hard time waiting for the microwave popcorn to finish popping!

But when God seems to hide himself from us, and when the light in our souls turns to dark night, every moment is agony. The pain of that loneliness can last days, weeks, even months, but God always returns. And he's always on time.

> I waited patiently for the LORD;
>> he inclined to me and heard my cry.
> He drew me up from the pit of destruction,
>> out of the miry bog,
> and set my feet upon a rock,
>> making my steps secure.

He put a new song in my mouth,
    a song of praise to our God.
Many will see and fear,
    and put their trust in the LORD. (Psalm 40:1–3)

Christians throughout history have waited patiently for the Lord and have been rewarded.

Robert Glover was a devout follower of Christ in England. In 1555 he was arrested for denying state-approved doctrine, tried for heresy, and sentenced to burn at the stake. Just days before his execution, however, Robert experienced God's dreadful withdrawal, and he fell into despair, fearing that God had abandoned his soul. One of Robert's friends, Austin, visited him in prison and encouraged him to stay patient and wait for God, saying that God would come back before the end.

The day before his death, Robert spent most of his time in prayer, but he still felt no presence or comfort from God. The next day, however, as his executioners led him to the stake, he suddenly felt God's presence so profoundly that he started clapping his hands in joy and crying out, "Oh, Austin, he has come! He has come!"

If you feel as if God has withdrawn his presence from you and your whole world is a spiritual dark night, be patient and trust him. He'll come back. And he'll remind you of his eternal love and the truth that he never really left you at all.

Yes, God's love for his children is eternal. I wrote this book so you can *know* that you know God and that you'll spend eternity with him. If you are truly a child of God, he wants you to experience that kind of certainty in your life today.

The Best Is Yet to Come

What does knowing I belong to God
promise for my eternity?

Wrong will be right, when Aslan comes in sight,
At the sound of his roar, sorrows will be no more,
When he bares his teeth, winter meets its death,
And when he shakes his mane, we shall have
spring again.

—C. S. LEWIS

In his book *The Problem of Pain,* C. S. Lewis wrote,

There have been times when I think we do not desire
heaven; but more often I find myself wondering whether,

in our heart of hearts, we have ever desired anything else.
It is the secret signature of each soul, the incommunicable
and unappeasable want, the thing we desired before we
met our wives or made our friends or chose our work,
and which we shall still desire on our deathbeds, when
the mind no longer knows wife, or friend, or work. All
your life an unattainable ecstasy has hovered just beyond
the grasp of your consciousness. The day is coming when
you will wake to find, beyond all hope, that you have
attained it.[1]

Lewis penned those words after the premature death of his
wife, Joy, and he put his finger on the hope possessed by all who
know God. The day is coming when God will satisfy our deepest
longings and fulfill our highest dreams. He'll wipe away all our
tears and end every frustration. He will, in the words of J. R. R.
Tolkien, make "everything sad come untrue." He'll right every
wrong and correct every injustice. The day is coming when we'll
work and play and worship forever, with no more sin, no more
sickness and disease, no more failure, no more pain, no more
death. There is coming a day when the kingdoms of this world
will become the kingdom of our Lord and of his Christ, and we
will reign with him forever and ever (Revelation 11:15).

When God enters into an everlasting relationship with you,
he fills you with the assurance and certainty that you will spend

eternity with him. We've explored how we can experience that assurance and certainty in this life. But where does it all lead? What does knowing God promise for our future? What does God have planned for those of us who can truly call him Father? It's at this point—the Christian's future hope—where finding certainty in life's most important relationship becomes most important.

As J. C. Ryle said, "A day is coming upon us all when the value of everything will be altered."

A day is coming when banknotes will be as useless as rags, and gold will be as worthless as the dust of the earth. A day is coming when thousands will care nothing for the things for which they once lived, and will desire nothing so much as the things which they once despised. The mansions and palaces will be forgotten in the desire of a "house not made with hands." The favor of the rich and great will be remembered no more, in the longing for the favor of the King of kings. The silks, and satins, and velvets, and laces, will be lost sight of in the anxious need of the robe of Christ's righteousness. All will be altered, all will be changed in the great day of the Lord's return.[2]

Permit me to ask you respectfully and lovingly one more time, do you know God?

Nothing Is Sound

I just came from the hospital where my sixty-seven-year-old father had open-heart surgery for the second time in four years. His doctors discovered that some of his valves weren't working well, so they decided to go back in and repair or replace his damaged valves. Heart surgery is fairly routine these days, but Dad's surgery took a lot longer than any of us expected. The surgeon said Dad came through the surgery well. But he added that Dad's heart is in worse condition than he had anticipated, and he'll be shocked if Dad lives another ten years.

I gasped. It was the first time I ever encountered the sobering reality that my dad will die one day. Ten years doesn't sound long at all, and the thought of losing him breaks my heart. Dad is one of my best friends and wisest advisors. I haven't made one major decision over the past fifteen years without seeking his counsel. He's also one of my biggest fans. No one encourages me more than my dad.

Thinking about living the rest of my life without my dad is sad. I can't imagine the loss I'll feel when he dies. But this experience reminds me of the fact that life and the world we live in aren't what they're supposed to be. This isn't the perfect world God created before we filled it with sin. There's something about diseased hearts, painful recoveries, death, and relational separation that sobers us up to the reality that things aren't right in our world.

In their song "Happy Is a Yuppie Word," the band Switchfoot sings, "Nothing is sound, nothing is right-side right." And it's true: everything is out of kilter. Our deepest instincts tell us that nothing is as it should be, that everything needs to be reordered and recalibrated. Regardless of our religion or political beliefs, we agree that we live in an imperfect world, a world marred by injustice, fear, deceit, pride, loss, violence, lust, greed, disease, and disaster.

I remember watching television footage of the devastation after Hurricane Katrina slammed into the southern coast of the United States. I was speechless. Thousands were presumed dead. Tens of thousands were homeless. They had no water, no ice, no milk, no eggs, no bread. They had no electricity, no phone service, no clothes, no transportation. One woman appeared on screen and tearfully lamented that she had lost her twelve-year-old son in the storm, and she didn't know where he was. Another ten-year-old boy lost his parents and all his siblings. Thousands of people lost everything they owned.

Yet while the storm's devastation was awful, worse were the scenes of evil and inhumanity. Thousands of people seeking refuge were trapped in the New Orleans Convention Center and the Superdome. In the confusion and desperation, some people turned on one another. Fights broke out; people were shot; women were raped and robbed. In some parts of the city, caregivers ignored the elderly and left them to die. Looters ransacked neighborhood stores. Politicians seemed more interested in pointing fingers and laying blame than in getting things done. Religious leaders, activists, and legal counselors all weighed in on how poorly the other guy handled things.

One night. One storm. One ugly display of what's wrong in this world.

"Wherever anything wrong exists in the world, anything we experience as anti-normative, evil, distorted, or sick, there we meet the perversion of God's good creation," said Albert Wolters.[3] That perversion started in a garden. Adam and Eve's disobedience was an act of cosmic treason that catastrophically diseased all of God's good creation. Humanity's revolt perverted everything God created—not only individual human beings, but all of nature and society as well.

Humanity's fall in Genesis 3 created a disharmony in nature that often makes the world a hostile place for all living things.

> The creation was subjected to futility, not willingly, but because of him who subjected it, in hope that the creation itself will be set free from its bondage to decay and obtain the freedom of the glory of the children of God. (Romans 8:20–21)

Without our sin, nature would be completely free from danger, chaos, calamity, and death.

Sin's effect on society is equally obvious. John Stott wrote:

> Much that we take for granted in a civilized society is based upon the assumption of human sin. A promise is not enough; we need a contract. Doors are not enough; we have to lock and bolt them. Law and order are not enough; we need the police to enforce them. All this is due to mankind's sin. We cannot trust each other. We need protection against one another.[4]

Because of sin, everything around us is decaying, dying, and coming to an end. But what if the atheists are right? What if this broken world is all there is? The apostle Paul said, "If in this life only we have hoped in Christ, we are of all people most to be pitied" (1 Corinthians 15:19). In other words, if this world is all we have and there's no hope for a world to come, we're doomed to lives of misery.

The Bible, however, tells us that Christians do have hope for a better world. Jesus said that he was leaving to prepare a place for us and that he would return one day to lead us there himself. What is this place Jesus is preparing for those who know God?

IS HEAVEN ALL THERE IS?

When I was boy, I was more interested in avoiding hell than in attaining heaven. I knew the Bible described hell as a place of pain and misery, so I knew I didn't want to go there. But to be honest, the alternative of heaven sounded boring. I thought heaven sounded a lot like a typical church service—a really long church service. We'd spend all day, every day, for all eternity, singing hymns, praying prayers, and listening to sermons. Come to think of it, my idea of heaven sounded a lot like hell to me.

I think that's one of the main reasons I decided not to follow God when I was young. The opportunities in this world seemed a lot more exciting than anything heaven had to offer. Don't get me wrong: I still didn't want to go to hell. Heaven might be boring, but I knew hell was a lot worse. So I set out to gain the best of both worlds. I decided I would go out and get all the excitement I could from this world, and when I'd had enough, I'd get serious with God again so I wouldn't go to hell when I died.

The problem is, I totally misunderstood what heaven is all about. Contrary to what I thought, heaven is not the ultimate destination for those who know God.

What?

That's right. I'll say it again: if you know God, heaven is not your ultimate destination.

Now, before you charge me with heresy, let me explain.

Those who know God are destined to go to heaven. But it's not our ultimate destination. This is what I mean.

When you die, your body (the physical part of you) goes into the ground while your soul (the nonphysical part of you) goes to be with the Lord. Jesus made that clear when he told the thief on the cross next to him, "Truly, I say to you, today you will be with me in Paradise" (Luke 23:43). And in 1 Corinthians 15, Paul taught that to be absent from the body is to be present with the Lord. For now, let's call this place where our souls go when we die "heaven." We continue to live a conscious existence there as disembodied spirits awaiting the final resurrection. In other words, heaven is our *intermediate* home.

To be sure, this heaven is better than our present earth. After all, heaven is where God is. Heaven is where the angels are. Heaven is without sin and pain and temptation and pressure. But believe it or not, as I said, God has better plans for us. So our stay in heaven is only temporary as we wait for the final resurrection.

What's the final resurrection?

When Jesus returns to earth someday, everybody who knows God—including all who have been living in heaven as disembodied spirits—will receive brand-new bodies. God will take our sinless souls and place them in perfect, sinless bodies. God will put us back together so we can enter our ultimate destination.

And the ultimate destination for those who truly know God is a new heaven *and* a new earth. Let me explain further.

New Bodies in a New World

The apostle Peter said, "According to his promise we are waiting for new heavens and a new earth in which righteousness dwells" (2 Peter 3:13). And the apostle John described this new heaven and earth:

> I saw a new heaven and a new earth, for the first heaven
> and the first earth had passed away, and the sea was no
> more. And I saw the holy city, new Jerusalem, coming
> down out of heaven from God, prepared as a bride
> adorned for her husband. And I heard a loud voice from
> the throne saying, "Behold, the dwelling place of God is
> with man. He will dwell with them, and they will be his
> people, and God himself will be with them as their God."
> (Revelation 21:1–3)

This means that one day all God's children will live in a new, sin-free, physical world with new, sin-free, physical bodies.

Still need proof? It rests in Christ's resurrection. "The central significance of Jesus's resurrection lies in the fact that it is just the beginning of the saving, renewing, resurrecting work of God that will have its climax in the restoration of the entire cosmos," wrote K. Scott Oliphant and Sinclair Ferguson.[5] And John Stott said the bodily resurrection of Jesus "was the first bit of material order to be redeemed and transfigured. It is the divine pledge that the rest will be redeemed and transfigured one day."[6]

When the Bible speaks about Jesus being the firstfruits of the harvest and the firstborn from the dead (Romans 8:29; 1 Corinthians 15:20, 23; Colossians 1:18; Revelation 1:5), it's speaking about the fact that Christ was the first to rise, and all his people will follow him someday. When the Apostles' Creed says, "We believe in the resurrection of the body," that's what it's talking about. It's talking about that day when Christ will return and place our sinless souls inside new sinless bodies so that we'll live forever, like him, in a perfect physical state.

And what will our brand-new, perfect, sinless bodies be like? The Bible doesn't give us specific details, but Paul said our bodies will be like Christ's resurrected body (Philippians 3:21) and they'll be imperishable, glorious, and powerful (1 Corinthians 15:42–44). We can be sure that these bodies will be able to do things our present bodies can't. We'll possess new and undreamed-of abilities.

I think I can also say with certainty that you're going to like the way you look. I'm sure most of us have issues with our bodies and how we look on the outside. But Paul said our perfect God will personally choose the perfect body for each one of his children (1 Corinthians 15:38).

Christ's resurrection not only guarantees us that perfect, new, disease-free bodies are on the way, but a new, sin-free world is on the way as well. Jesus said that when he returns, he will not only raise the dead, but he will also heal and restore the entire universe (Matthew 19:28), "making all things new" (Revelation 21:5). In this new creation, the Bible says, we'll see trees that dance, colors we've never seen, and places we've never been. But at the same time, we'll rediscover things we *have* seen and places we *have* been. "We will meet all kinds of new people and see all kinds of new places," says Randy Alcorn. "But we will also see familiar people and familiar places, because we will be with resurrected people we love on the resurrected Earth we love."[7]

But if God is creating a new heaven and a new earth, what will he do with our present earth? Some Bible scholars interpret verses such as 2 Peter 3:7 and Luke 21:33 to mean that God plans to destroy our present world—all of it—and start over, creating a new world from scratch. The Bible, however, also talks about creation waiting for its ultimate redemption and renewal.

> The creation waits with eager longing for the revealing of the sons of God. For the creation was subjected to futility, not willingly, but because of him who subjected it, in hope that the creation itself will be set free from its bondage to decay and obtain the freedom of the glory of the children of God. (Romans 8:19–21)

In other words, God doesn't plan to build a brand-new world from scratch. Instead, he plans a radical renovation project of the world we live in today.

God won't destroy everything that now exists, but he will destroy all the corruption, brokenness, and chaos we see in our world, purging from it everything that is impure and sinful. He did something like this once before. Remember the Flood in Genesis 6–9? God flooded his creation and washed away everything that was perverse and wicked. But he did not obliterate everything. In the same way, when it comes to the new heaven and new earth, God won't annihilate our present world; he'll renew, redeem, and resurrect it. "We will be the same people made new and we will live on the same Earth made new," Alcorn wrote.[8]

Right now we live in what C. S. Lewis called "the shadowlands." Everything in this earth is a pale reflection of what things will one day be like. But in God's new world, we'll rediscover all the places we used to enjoy, minus the sin, brokenness, and corruption. There will be no more death, no more decay.

I so look forward to that day, returning to God's remade world to see what he's done to all my favorite places. It's hard to imagine how God could possibly improve on the Grand Canyon, the Swiss Alps, a desert sunset, or a clear night with diamonds twinkling in the sky. But I think what I most want to see again is the ocean.

I love the ocean and the beach. I love everything about them: the warm Florida water, the calming sound of the waves, the soft sand, the hot sun on my skin. My family and I live just fifteen minutes from the beach, and we go almost every Saturday to surf and play in the sand. I can't wait to see God's perfect new ocean. I can't even imagine a more perfect sun, warming perfect water, and me riding perfect waves in God's new world.

Like an unborn child in the womb, God's new world is waiting to be born. And like a pregnant woman, nature groans with labor pains like tornadoes, hurricanes, floods, tsunamis, and volcanic eruptions. "We know that the whole creation has been groaning together in the pains of childbirth until now," Paul wrote in Romans 8:22. But those labor pains promise the birth of a new world. Amazing!

I know what labor pains look like. When my wife gave birth to our three children, I stayed in the delivery room with her each time. I agonized over the pain she endured, but she says that each painful contraction carried the promise that new life was on the way. Despite the agony she went through each time, what we gained was worth it all—the miraculous birth of a beautiful child.

It's a wonderful picture, isn't it? We're all living in God's delivery room, watching all of creation groaning in labor. Paul said in Romans 8:20–23 that each chaotic act of nature is another painful contraction promising the birth of a brand-new world where we will one day spend eternity with God our Father. New bodies in a new world—this is the ultimate destination for those who know God.

ONE DAY

My friend West, who lives in Tennessee with his wife and daughter, sent me this e-mail:

> When I picked up Abby today from her first day of school, I noticed along the wall outside her class the work the children had done: smiley faces on paper plates stapled to Popsicle sticks. Oddly, Abby's was a frown. At the same time across town Suzanne was finding out that the child in her womb had gone to be with the Lord. It is a sad day for us, and I'm sure these tears will soak our pillows tonight.
>
> We know it shouldn't be this way. Every ounce of our being knows it. Our hearts are so profoundly enlightened in times of pain. We realize we were not created for grief, but joy; not death, but life!
>
> Thanks be to God, though, that we do not grieve as those without hope. The Lord gives and the Lord takes away. Blessed be the name of the Lord (Job 1:21).

After I wiped the tears from my eyes, this was my response:

Dearest West,

I love you. I am crying with you. I don't know what to say.

"I long to be where the praise is never ending; yearn to dwell where the glory never fades."

One day, my friend, one day…[9]

Do you know God? If not, then God the Father invites you to join his family today and to spend eternity with him in a brand-new world as his adopted child. He promises that if you surrender your life to him and bow your knee before Jesus, he will love you forever, and nothing—*nothing*—can ever change that. Yes, you *can* know God. And he will certainly give you the inheritance that Christ earned for sinners like you and me: "For God so loved the world, that he gave his only Son, that whoever believes in him should not perish but have eternal life" (John 3:16).

As Blaise Pascal discovered almost 350 years ago:

"Certainty, certainty, heartfelt, joy, peace"!

Acknowledgments

There is nothing glamorous about writing a book. In fact, it can get downright ugly at times. I could never have started, much less completed, this project without the help of many. So I'd like to express gratitude to some who have accompanied me on this arduous eighteen-month journey.

To my friend Josh Harris, who was the first to suggest that I put my ideas into print. Remember that night at my grandparents' house, Josh? We stayed up late talking in the kitchen, and you persuaded me to start writing books. You even got the ball rolling by contacting your publisher on my behalf. Thanks, Josh!

To Kevin Marks, who, on Josh's recommendation, contacted me and asked me to consider writing for Multnomah. You then flew across the country to spend a day with me in South Florida to talk about life, books, and contracts while a tropical storm was making its way toward us. Thank you, Kevin (and Multnomah), for your interest and support from the beginning.

To David Kopp, who has become like a literary father to me. You helped me get this book started, and you helped me get this book finished. From beginning to end, you have been my guide, my support, and my cheerleader. Thanks also for enduring my fits (and late-night phone calls) from time to time. You're a patient man!

To Larry (L. A.) Wilson, what can I say? You taught me more about writing in six weeks than I had learned in thirty-four years. Your humility, patience, skill with words, and willingness to correct me helped me find my voice. You assisted me in turning something messy into something meaningful. Thanks, Larry!

To John Frame, Mark Futato, Carolyn Nystrom, Maurice Roberts, Jimmy Branham, Scott Cochran, J. I. Packer, Os Guinness, Ravi Zacharias, Danielle DuRant, Mark Dever, and David Wells. All of you read portions of this manuscript (in its roughest form) and offered encouraging endorsements, probing suggestions, and helpful corrections. What a community of friends and mentors God has given me!

To my New City Church family. I love you all so much. Thank you for allowing me to be your pastor and for supporting me along the way. Your strong encouragement keeps me preaching (which keeps me writing). Thank you. Thank God.

To Brandon, Dylan, Paul, Lana, Kristin, Deanna, Wendy, Mark, John, Jeff, Jim, Milan, and Steve for helping to cover my bases while I was busy writing. It is a privilege serving with you. New City is a strong, healthy, thriving young church because of your God-centered devotion. You are the best friends I've ever had.

To Daddy Bill for writing the foreword. I can't believe the heritage God has given me. Because of your faithfulness to Jesus for more than sixty years, my children and my children's children will be blessed. You have been one of my closest friends and most reliable counselors all my life. I want to be just like you when I grow up.

To my children, Gabe, Nate, and Genna. I'll never be able to adequately express just how much I love you all. You were so patient with me while I was writing this book. So many times you wanted me to play, and I couldn't, and you were kind enough to understand. It is a joy to be your dad. Seriously!

To my wife, Kim. I am certain that no one sacrificed more during this time than you. You are the love of my life, the wife of my youth, and the apple of my eye. God knew exactly what he was doing when he brought you to me. Apart from God saving me, you are, hands down, the best thing that has ever happened to me. I love you, honey!

And to my Lord and Savior Jesus Christ, who gave everything that I might possess all. You are my everlasting King. Thank you for saving me, loving me, and promising me that the best is yet to come. All that I am and all that I have belongs to you—including this book. I pray that it serves to spread your glorious fame. It's all about you!

Study Guide
for Personal and Group Use

Chapter 1: The Hope of Certainty
Is knowing God really possible?

"I meet people almost every day who are struggling with whether God is knowable," writes the author, "and, if he is, what it means to have a relationship with him." And considering the outcomes connected with whether we know God, the quest is clearly an important one. In an uncertain world, being sure that we do know God might seem too much to hope for. But the Bible shows that humans are, in fact, created to know God. Not only can we know God, but we can also be certain that we do (2 Peter 1:10).

1. Based on what you know and feel now, which statement on the following scale of knowing God with certainty most accurately describes you?
   a. I know God with certainty, and I know why I know.
   b. I'm pretty sure I know God, and I have reasons to believe I'm probably correct.

    c. Sometimes I think (or feel) that I know God; some-
       times I don't.

    d. I'm pretty sure I *don't* know God, although I'd love to
       be wrong.

    e. I know I do not know God.

2. When it comes to knowing God, do you think some
people are more comfortable *not* knowing for sure where
they stand? If so, why do you think that might be true?

3. Read Romans 1:18–20; 2 Timothy 3:16–17; and Hebrews 1:1–4 in your Bible. What forms of self-revelation
by God do you find described in these verses? What pro-
gression do you see among these forms in terms of the
fullness of divine revelation? How do you think they can
help you in *knowing* that you know God?

4. Read 2 Corinthians 13:5 in its context. More is to come
in Tullian's book about examining one's faith and testing
whether it is true or not. But at this stage, what do you
think it means to "examine [yourself], to see whether
you are in the faith"?

5. Tullian describes a "rigorous personal inventory" ahead
in *Do I Know God?* If you were to fully engage in this
inventory, what do you think God's attitude and
response might be toward you in the process? On what
do you base your answer?

Chapter 2: Real Relationship with God
What does it mean to truly know God?

Knowing *about* someone and truly *knowing* that person are different—a Grand Canyon of difference, observes the author. To know God, we must cross the canyon of sin and separation, but we can't do that on our own. Thankfully, Jesus Christ has bridged the chasm for sinners. Through him, sinners can now be brought close to God—adopted as sons and daughters into our heavenly Father's family. As new creatures in Christ, Christians can rest in the unalterable, external fact of their secure relationship to God (eternal security) while also experiencing the internal awareness of its authenticity (assurance of salvation).

1. Tullian states that "Christianity is first and foremost about a relationship to God." Is this how you would define Christianity? If not, how would you describe it?
2. Read John 1:12–13; Romans 8:14–16; and Galatians 4:1–7. How do these passages fill out your understanding of adoption as a son or daughter of God?
3. Explain the difference between eternal security and assurance of salvation in your own words.
4. What is eternal security based upon? On whom does it depend? (You may wish to refer to Romans 8:31–39;

Philippians 1:6; 1 Peter 1:3–5, and other Bible passages
for help in answering.)

5. Tullian believes firmly that if you have a relationship
with God, he wants you to know it (1 John 5:13). What
benefits can come to a Christian who experiences a deep
assurance of salvation?

Chapter 3: Avoiding the Many
*How can I be sure that I am not deceived by the false certainty the
Bible warns about?*

This chapter opens with Jesus's story of those who thought they
knew the Lord but actually did not (Matthew 7:21–23). Notice,
says Tullian, that Jesus described this group as "many." What could
lead to such a troubling—and devastating—misunderstanding?
Tullian examines two causes: the mistaken ideas that a repeated
prayer guarantees relationship to God and that the memory of a
past event or decision guarantees it. He concludes, "None of us
enters into a relationship with God merely by raising a hand,
praying a sinner's prayer, walking an aisle, or remembering a decision made years ago, especially if our lives show no evidence that
our prayer or decision made any difference."

1. What does false assurance mean in the context of this
book?

2. Tullian points to the un-Christian behavior of so-called Christians as a major source of disillusionment for believers and unbelievers alike. To what degree has this phenomenon been a factor in your own spiritual experience? How have you dealt with it in the past?

3. One example of the "many" false followers of Jesus is Judas Iscariot. Read Matthew 10:1–4. What kinds of spiritual activities did Judas presumably participate in? Read Matthew 26:20–25. How did Jesus characterize Judas's eventual behavior and its consequences? How do you account for the contradictions in Judas's life?

4. Can you be truly assured that you have a relationship with God based only on your praying a prayer or walking an aisle? Why or why not?

5. Can you be truly assured that you have a relationship with God based only on your remembering a time when you made a decision for Christ? Why or why not?

Chapter 4: The Promise of Proximity
Does being sincerely religious or spiritual mean I know God?

No wonder earnest religiosity or spirituality feels like a sure bet to getting a person close to God: the sole purpose of these ancient paths is to bring us near to God. But nearness is not the same thing as knowing, according to the Bible. Religion and spirituality are human-centered efforts to reach God that leave us thirsty for his presence. Writes Tullian, "Only true relationship with God through faith in Jesus Christ can satisfy [our spiritual] thirst."

1. Why do you think people so often confuse having religious attitudes and behaviors with having a relationship to God?

2. Why do you think people so often confuse New Age or other forms of spirituality with having a relationship to God?

3. The apostles battled pointless religiosity inside the church and baseless spirituality outside. Read Acts 15:1–11 and 17:22–31, and identify the deceptions people were laboring under. How do these biblical incidents remind you of mistaken beliefs held by people you know?

4. What reasons could you suggest to explain why these two deceptions about how to know God are so deeply rooted in America and around the world?

5. Based on your own experience, to what degree would you say these two deceptions can thrive even in a Bible-teaching and Bible-living church? Why?

Chapter 5: Working *For,* Working *Out*
What is the relationship between saving faith and good works?

Writes Tullian of a friend's father, "Cliff…was one of the kindest, gentlest men I have ever known." Yet a deep conviction seemed to prevent him from receiving God's free offer of salvation in Jesus Christ. In this chapter the author wrestles with the desire of most spiritually sincere persons to win God's approval (and thereby a relationship with him) by doing good works. But it is an approval that Christ has already won at the cross. Then Tullian explores the relationship between saving faith in Christ and the good works that must accompany this faith.

1. Based on your understanding of human nature, what common shortcoming(s) would you say might have hindered Cliff from knowing God?
2. Review Philippians 2:12–13. What does the passage say about the "work" we do and the "work" God does?
3. How have you seen people fall into the two deceptions that Tullian describes in this chapter?
4. What is the relationship between saving faith and good works? In your own words, describe how Paul and James spoke differently about this relationship (Galatians 2:15–16; James 2:14–26).

5. As candidly as possible, describe your normal motivations for doing good works.

Chapter 6: The Weight of His Word

How does believing God's promises assure me of my salvation?

You can trust a promise only as much as you know and trust the person making the promise. Can you know and trust God in the same way? Data show that American Christians who say "In God we trust" may not know him well at all. In this chapter the author lays down the biblical evidence for a God who is independent, immutable, and infinite—a God of flawless character who can be trusted to keep his promises regarding what it means to know him.

1. How does God's character make him trustworthy? Which attributes or actions of God, if any, still leave you with questions?

2. Scan Hebrews 11, and choose a hero who, for you, epitomizes trust in God. If you can find his or her story in the Old Testament, read it. What about this person inspires you to trust God's promises?

3. How are God's promises about relationship related to the person and work of Jesus Christ? In what way do all of them hinge upon the person and work of Jesus? (See 2 Corinthians 1:20.)

4. From what does God promise to save those who place their faith in what Jesus accomplished on the cross? What does God promise to save them to?

5. Do you trust the character of God? Do you believe his promises? Why or why not?

Chapter 7: A Sense of the Presence
How do my feelings for God assure me of my salvation?

In this chapter the author turns from outward facts to inward experiences and a rigorous examination of motivations and desires. He writes, "When God becomes your most passionate desire, you will find growing certainty in life's most important relationship." Along with thoughts, feelings matter to Christians because God redeems both and is ready to be known by both. We are to be those who can say, "As a deer pants for flowing streams, so pants my soul for you, O God" (Psalm 42:1).

1. Tullian begins this chapter with a description of a visit at his grandparents' log cabin, where God's presence always seems powerfully present. Could you point to a person or persons who have influenced your life in a similar way? Describe their character, behavior, or environment. What factors about them or their home speak most convincingly to you of God's presence?

2. While the Christian faith is based on fact, finding certainty in our relationship to God is also tied to our desires. If you have become a Christian, how has God changed your desires?

3. Do you tend to be more intellectual or more emotional in your pursuit of God? What are some hazards to your tendency? How could you grow in loving God more in your weaker area?

4. The blending of heart and mind for the Christian is a consistent theme of Scripture. How do Matthew 22:37; John 4:23–24; 1 Corinthians 14:15; and Ephesians 4:15 challenge you?

5. What would you say is at the center of your affections? What do you love most? For example, what in your life would you describe by saying, "If I didn't have this, I could not live happily"?

Chapter 8: Outward Evidence of Inward Events
How does obedience to God assure me of my salvation?

Relationship to God is a work of God—a fact that he accomplishes for his adopted children. But fellowship with God is largely up to us—a priority to protect and pursue, in the same way that fellowship with extended family depends on effort. Writes Tullian, "The

Bible says that we pursue fellowship with God by obeying him."
What follows is a discussion about how sin and obedience in the
Christian—though covered by the blood of Christ—wreak havoc
in our lives, pollute our spirits, stunt our growth, and soil our experience of God's presence and favor. Obedience, by contrast, gives
evidence that we are truly in relationship to God.

1. What is the difference between having a relationship to
   God and enjoying fellowship with God? How is relationship connected to eternal security? How is fellowship connected to assurance of salvation?
2. What should be our motive for obeying God? (See John
   14:15.)
3. Read 1 John 2:3–6. What makes obeying the Lord a
   reliable form of evidence that we know God?
4. Give some thought to how you react when you sin.
   Describe what emotions and concerns typically follow.
   Do you feel guilt, remorse, regret? Are you concerned
   with what God thinks of your sin? What are the short-
   and long-term consequences of disobedience, in your
   experience?
5. How has your behavior changed since you came to
   Christ? What further steps of obedience would you say
   you've been neglecting and need to make?

Chapter 9: The Practical Pursuit of Assurance

What can I do to experience the assurance of salvation?

This chapter puts practical steps to the big idea of the previous chapter—that obedience enhances our assurance of salvation. Healthy relationships flourish with tender care and languish without it. In our relationship to God, three areas that call for spiritual attention are Bible reading, prayer, and commitment to the church. As Scripture says, "Draw near to God, and he will draw near to you" (James 4:8).

1. Read the following Bible passages and summarize what they teach: Psalm 119:33–38; Luke 11:1–13; Ephesians 2:19–22.

2. How does reading the Bible and hearing it taught help us in our relationship to God? Despite the benefits, many Christians admit to feeling intimidated or less than motivated by the Bible. How would you describe your attitude toward the Bible?

3. What is prayer? Why is it important? What practical steps can you take to improve your prayer life?

4. Why is being an active part of a local church important? What does Tullian mean when he says the church is the "communal arena of grace"? Are you devoted to a local church?

5. What are the interruptions and hindrances that most often keep you from the practical disciplines of growing in your relationship to God? How do you typically respond? What one thing could you change this week that would bring an immediate, measurable improvement?

Chapter 10: Knowing God in the Dark Night

How can I be assured of God's presence when what I feel most is his absence?

Asks Tullian, "What about those seasons in life when we draw near to God, but he doesn't draw near to us, at least as far as we can tell?" God's children down through the centuries have experienced the tortures of God's apparent distance, detachment, and silence. This distressing experience, writes Tullian, can actually be a comfort, because we wouldn't so dearly miss what was not so deeply real. And it's in these times when we learn to wait, trust, and live by faith.

1. Have you experienced times when God seemed far away? Describe how you felt during that time. Could you trace it to anything amiss in your life or surroundings? Or did it seem that God withdrew for his own reasons?

2. Bible scholars believe Psalms 42 and 43 may have originally been a single work. Scan these two psalms and answer: How does the psalmist express his sense of separation from God? How does he express his desire for God? What does he ask of God? How does he hold on to hope?

3. In relation to God, do you think absence makes the heart grow fonder or makes the heart to wander? How can you encourage the former and prevent the latter?

4. Why is it so hard to trust God when we cannot trace him? Take some time to reflect on all the ways God has taken care of you. How could that reflection enhance your trust in God's goodness when he seems absent?

5. Why is waiting on God so hard (Psalm 37:7)? Yet why is waiting necessary when we are experiencing a dark night of the soul?

Chapter 11: The Best Is Yet to Come
What does knowing I belong to God promise for my eternity?

By far the greatest benefit of knowing God now is that we will also know him for all eternity. Unfortunately, many Christians live with an inaccurate and unattractive vision of their destiny after death. Jesus promised his followers a better place than this broken planet. Tullian closes his study of what it means to know

God by showing a biblical view of the new heaven and new earth that await all God's sons and daughters.

1. Writes Tullian, "The day is coming when God will satisfy our deepest longings and fulfill our highest dreams." Describe the longings and dreams that you think may not be fulfilled until eternity.

2. How has sin affected humanity's ability to experience the best that relationship can offer? (See Romans 8:18–25.)

3. What is the final resurrection? (See 1 Corinthians 15:12–58.) On what is the final resurrection grounded? How do we know it will happen? How does the promise of a new body and a new world compare with what you've been taught before?

4. Look over the poetic description of the new heavens and new earth in Revelation 21:1–22:5. Which details whet your appetite for resurrection life the most, and why?

5. How could a settled assurance about your everlasting relationship with God affect your day today—your choices, your moods, your courage?

Notes

Chapter One: The Hope of Certainty

1. Blaise Pascal, *Pensées,* trans. A. J. Krailsheimer (London: Penguin Books, 1995), 285–86.

2. Blaise Pascal, *Aflame with Love: Selections from the Writings of Blaise Pascal,* comp. Robert E. Coleman (Minneapolis: WorldWide Publications, 1974), 17.

3. R. C. Sproul, *Essential Truths of the Christian Faith* (Wheaton, IL: Tyndale, 1992), 32.

4. J. I. Packer, *Hot Tub Religion: Christian Living in a Materialistic World* (Wheaton, IL: Tyndale, 1987), 25.

5. Fanny Crosby, "Blessed Assurance."

Chapter Two: Real Relationship with God

1. J. I. Packer, *Concise Theology: A Guide to Historic Christian Beliefs* (Wheaton, IL: Tyndale, 1993), 82.

2. Shannon Baker, "Chapman Sees Adoption as the 'Visible Gospel,'" *Baptist Life,* November 1, 2004.

3. John R. W. Stott, *Men with a Message* (London: Longmans, 1954), 126.

4. Billy Graham, *Peace with God* (Minneapolis: Grason, 1984), 219.

5. Joseph Hart, "Come Ye Sinners, Poor and Needy."

Chapter Three: Avoiding the Many

1. Donald S. Whitney, *How Can I Be Sure I'm a Christian? What the Bible Says About Assurance of Salvation* (Colorado Springs, CO: NavPress, 1994), 115–16.

2. Charles Wesley, "And Can It Be That I Should Gain?"

Chapter Four: The Promise of Proximity

1. See Don W. Robertson, *The Christian Sabbath* (Coulterville, IL: New Creation Publications, 2001).

2. Isaac Watts, "When I Survey the Wondrous Cross."

3. For a more detailed discussion of our culture's increasing fascination with things spiritual, I recommend David F. Wells, *Above All Earthly Pow'rs: Christ in a Postmodern World* (Grand Rapids: Eerdmans, 2005).

4. For a detailed outworking of this idea, see Peter L. Berger and Richard John Neuhaus, eds., *Against the World for the World: The Hartford Appeal and the Future of American Religion* (New York: Seabury, 1976).

5. N. T. Wright, *Simply Christian: Why Christianity Makes Sense* (New York: HarperCollins, 2006), 25.

Chapter Five: Working For, Working Out

1. Gerrit Scott Dawson, *Jesus Ascended: The Meaning of Christ's Continuing Incarnation* (Phillipsburg, NJ: P & R Publishing, 2004), 124.

Chapter Six: The Weight of His Word

1. Byron Johnson and others, "Losing My Religion? No, Says Baylor Religion Survey," September 11, 2006, Baylor Institute for Studies of Religion, Waco, Texas.

2. Richard L. Pratt Jr., *Every Thought Captive* (Phillipsburg, NJ: P & R Publishing, 1979), 17.

3. R. C. Sproul, *One Holy Passion: The Consuming Thirst to Know God* (Nashville: Thomas Nelson, 1987), 18.

4. John R. W. Stott, *The Contemporary Christian: Applying God's Word to Today's World* (Leicester, England: InterVarsity Press, 1992), 82.

5. C. S. Lewis, *Mere Christianity* (New York: HarperCollins, 2001), 216.

Chapter Seven: A Sense of the Presence

1. John Piper, *When I Don't Desire God: How to Fight for Joy* (Wheaton, IL: Crossway, 2004), 31.

2. J. C. Ryle, *Practical Religion* (Grand Rapids: Baker, 1977), 11.

3. F. W. Faber, quoted in Ralph G. Turnbull, *A Minister's Obstacles* (1946; repr., Grand Rapids: Baker, 1972), 97.

Chapter Eight: Outward Evidence of Inward Events

1. John R. W. Stott, *Basic Christianity* (Downers Grove, IL: InterVarsity Press, 1958), 135.
2. John Murray, *Redemption Accomplished and Applied* (Grand Rapids: Eerdmans, 1955), 145.
3. Henry Martyn, "Journals and Letters of the Rev. Henry Martyn," June 1, Project Canterbury, http//anglicanhistory .org/india/martyn/1804.html.

Chapter Nine: The Practical Pursuit of Assurance

1. Many good books can help you be more intentional and disciplined in your relationship with God. I recommend *Spiritual Disciplines for the Christian Life* by Donald S. Whitney, *The Spirit of the Disciplines* by Dallas Willard, and *Disciplines of Grace* by T. M. Moore.
2. T. M. Moore, *Disciplines of Grace: From Spiritual Routines to Spiritual Renewal* (Downers Grove, IL: InterVarsity Press, 2001), 45–46.
3. Purchase this plan at www.navpress.com/Store/Product/ 1576839745.html.

Chapter Ten: Knowing God in the Dark Night

1. See, for instance, Psalms 6, 10, 13, 42, 63, and 69. In terms of a person's disposition, there is a huge difference between complaining and lamenting. Complaining is a cry *against* God; lamenting is a cry *for* God. Complaining is self-centered; lamenting is God-centered. To complain is to cry *against* God's providence; to lament is to cry *over* God's providence. Therefore, complaining is always a sin, while lamenting is not.

2. Larry Crabb, *Finding God* (Grand Rapids: Zondervan, 1993), 11.

3. J. I. Packer, ed., *Puritan Papers* (Phillipsburg, NJ: P & R Publishing, 2000), 1:36.

Chapter Eleven: The Best Is Yet to Come

1. C. S. Lewis, *The Problem of Pain* (New York: Macmillan, 1962), 145.

2. J. C. Ryle, *Practical Religion* (1883; repr., Grand Rapids: Baker, 1977), 40.

3. Albert M. Wolters, *Creation Regained: Biblical Basics for a Reformational Worldview* (Grand Rapids: Eerdmans, 1985), 46.

4. John R. W. Stott, *Basic Christianity* (Downers Grove, IL: InterVarsity Press, 1958), 135.

5. K. Scott Oliphant and Sinclair B. Ferguson, *If I Should Die Before I Wake: What's Beyond This Life?* (Fearn, Scotland: Christian Focus, 2004), 71.
6. John R. W. Stott, *The Contemporary Christian: Applying God's Word to Today's World* (Leicester, England: InterVarsity Press, 1992), 85.
7. Randy Alcorn with Linda Washington, *Heaven for Kids* (Carol Stream, IL: Tyndale, 2006), 56.
8. Alcorn with Washington, *Heaven for Kids,* 53.
9. In my e-mail I quoted "Beautiful Savior" by Stuart Townend.

Topical Index